KNITTING AROUND

Books by Elizabeth Zimmermann:

KNITTING WITHOUT TEARS *1971 Scribner's / Macmillan*

KNITTER'S ALMANAC *1975 Scribner's / Dover*

KNITTING WORKSHOP *1981 Schoolhouse Press*

KNITTING AROUND *1989 Schoolhouse Press*

Video Series' by Elizabeth Zimmermann

BUSY KNITTER *1965 PBS*

BUSY KNITTER II *1968 PBS*

KNITTING WORKSHOP *1981 Schoolhouse Video*

KNITTING GLOSSARY *1985 Schoolhouse Video*

WOOL GATHERING *1989 Schoolhouse Video*

KNITTING AROUND

or

KNITTING WITHOUT a LICENSE

By

Elizabeth Zimmermann

Edited By

Meg Swansen

Schoolhouse Press
Pittsville
Wisconsin

First Printing, September 1989

Second printing, May 1990

Third printing, May 1994

Fourth printing, March 1997

Fifth printing, March 2000

Sixth printing, June 2001

ISBN 0-942018-03-6

Published by
Schoolhouse Press
6899 Cary Bluff
Pittsville, WI 54466
(715) 884-2799

As well as publishing knitting books and
producing instructional knitting videos,
Schoolhouse Press supplies handknitters with
a full range of tools and materials. We will be
pleased to send you a catalogue upon request.

To the knitter, and to the Swansens
of which Meg and Liesl are both.
And to my darling Gaffer.

KNITTING AROUND
is the companion book to the
WOOL GATHERING
Video Series
starring
Elizabeth Zimmermann & Meg Swansen

Contents

*All of the above subjects are available for purchase as individual cassettes (**VHS only**) by writing to Schoolhouse Press.*

All of the wools, knitting tools, and knitting books mentioned in this book, as well as a large selection of other titles and materials are also available from Schoolhouse Press.

All of the garments shown in this book and in the videos have been knitted by Elizabeth and Meg.

Illustrations

All Knitting Drawings, Pencil Drawings and Watercolors
   by Elizabeth Zimmermann

"Knitchart" font for color-pattern graphs, courtesy
of Sidna Farley

Photo Credits

Chapter One, page 6 - <u>Woman's Day</u>

Chapter One, page 10 - Tom Zimmermann

Chapter Two, page 16 - Bernat

Chapter Five, page 103 - Alice Hess

Chapter Six, page 115 - Viking Press

Chapter Seven, page 130 - Mary Mann

Chapter Nine, page 177 - Diane Brady

Chapter Nine, page 181 - Tom Zimmermann

Back Cover, black & white - Dan Young

Front & Back Cover, color - Chris Swansen

Color Insert, pages 81 - 96 - Chris Swansen

All other knitting photos - Schoolhouse Press

All other **Digression** photos - Zimmermann Family Albums

KNITTING AROUND

Table of Contents

Table of Contents (continued)

*   *   *   *   *   *   *   *   *   *   *   *   *   *

Foreword
by
Elaine Rowley
Publisher and Editor of
KNITTER'S magazine

The gulf that separates those who knit and those who don't is only a few hours, or a few pages. But, to cross it, you need to know that you can. You need a knitter.

Like many, I'm a first generation knitter. My mother knit a bit in college, but not after; my grandmother didn't. No one I knew knitted except a far-away aunt. So I tried too hard, made it complicated, was frustrated, criticized, and stymied. Yarn, needles, and books disappeared into a bottom drawer with my other great undones.

Then one fall while at home on the farm, I found Elizabeth Zimmermann's *The Busy Knitter* on TV. My guess is that the result would have been the same had I first met Elizabeth in print: instant recognition that *knitting makes sense*. I had found my knitter. She may not have known it, but I was there at her knee for many years.

That was the important part, but the unimportant part makes a better story. *The Busy Knitter* kept us all busy. My mother and I located real wool and circular needles and began to knit our Scandinavian sweaters. Knitting the assigned inches was not as difficult as locating next week's telecast: this was in the early days of South Dakota Public TV, and they played hide-and-seek with the audience, but we managed. Soon we had sleeves and body knit to the underarms and eagerly awaited the next step. (Yes, mystery had returned to knitting: how would this all become a sweater?) But the next week was all seek and no find: no show; the station said, "No more cans." While we weren't exactly sure what that meant, it seemed to mean that although surely Elizabeth Zimmermann was busily knitting somewhere, she would not be doing it in our living room. Well, at least we had become knitters. And The Sweaters were tucked in the top drawer this time - higher hopes for *them.*

Next Fall, when the series started again, so did we. Soon we were back at the armholes and then safely past. The series was complete and so were our sweaters. Even better, Elizabeth's address flashed on the screen, and we could write off for more. Soon we had her at our fingertips: *Newsletters*, followed by *Knitting Without Tears* and then *Wool Gatherings.*

I remember the only time that I read while driving was on a spring morning down narrow old highway 77. I had just gotten *Knitter's Almanac* in the mail, and I could not wait. Fortunately, it was so foggy that no one else was on the road. Ah, youth. Anyway, the words were lapped up (mostly when not behind the wheel), wonderful words, and just enough of them. That's one of Elizabeth's secrets: she doesn't tell us too much; she leaves room to question, to think, and grow.

For many of the current crop of knitters, Elizabeth got the word out. For me it was perfect:

the basics - which still are only cast on, knit, purl, increase, decrease, and bind off;

an economic use of technique - a few, carefully chosen and applied with ingenuity;

the math boiled down to essential relationships - stitches and/or rows to inches, knitting measurements to body measurements (or whatever is being covered) parts to the whole;

a strong sense of what knitting can do and a dedication to making it do as much of the job as possible;

in service of this, an innovative and sculptural sense of design - all delivered as a good story, with wit, humor, and as much attention paid to my knitting mind as my knitting hands.

There are many useful books; author/authorities abound. But, once you have a working vocabulary, the dictionary is not the book through which you browse most often. For a good read, turn to Elizabeth.

I knit today because of Elizabeth. Had I not found her, perhaps I would have bumped into some other knee, but then again . . . A Knitter, a yarn shop, a magazine, a family, might not have been. Perhaps this book should come with a warning: "Caution, reading this may change your life." Read dangerously.

KNITTING AROUND

Author's Preface

What makes a bookwriter write a book? Precious little, as far as I'm concerned. It could be one of the many thoughts that cross the mind when one is reading someone else's book...especially, for instance, while knitting around. Really, handknitting is a dreamy activity, built into many people's thumbs and fingers by genes already there, itching to display their skills and achievement possibilities. My mother and her family belonged to generations of knitters. I personally prefer handknitting for its extreme portability, and its consequent implication of industry, if for no other virtues.

What is your current knitting project? Are you working in wool, silk, linen or cotton? The choice was up to you, and the materials tantamount to uncountable, depending on source, color, and texture. In short, Knitting Around is not only soothing and productive, but endowed with endless possibilities. The narrowest sleeves, mittens or socks may be constructed on four double-pointed needles, round and round; the most generous circular shawls or tablecloths with thousands of stitches around the perimeter on a longer circular needle. Accentuate your circular knitting with safety-pins, so that they alert you to the time and places for shaping, buttonholes, pattern repeats, pockets, etc.

The more I knit, the stronger becomes my taste for "dedicated" techniques (the "right" technique for the right job), and shaping. Knitting around enables me to watch the progress and ultimate appearance of my knitted project, and frequently decides - or suggests - the next move, without warning.

Funny how most knitters prefer knitting to purling. I think its because they learned knitting first and have its movements firmly implanted in their fingers, no matter in which hand they hold the wool. I'm pretty sure that if they had learned these techniques simultaneously, or learned to purl *first*, they would not prefer one to the other, as so many of us do.

Lately there has been a stimulating and intoxicating resurgence of textured stitch-patterns, as in, for instance, European traditional knitted garments: the Arans, Guernseys, Bavarian and Austrian folk jackets - all with their cables, zigzags, ornate ribbings, and other methods of mixing basic knit and purl to result in all manner of twists, turns, bobbles, gaps, braids and borders. What were the true origins of these manifestations? I can think of no genuine "mistake" which, if repeated at regular intervals, cannot become an impressive and possibly hitherto unknown design (and you'd better write down how you did it; these knitting manifestations are hard to remember and/or analyze after their initial birth). I have even found a use for what I formerly thought was the only true"mistake" in knitting: a split stitch. Now when I knit with 2 un-spun strands of that unique, hairy, Icelandic wool, I am liable to deliberately split a stitch when I want to increase...knit into one strand, then into the other.

Why bother? Of course, if dreaming up a "new" piece of handknitting texture hurts the brain, ignore it. If it turns up accidently in a piece of knitting done yesterday, try and neutralize your attitude to it. Perhaps you are an instinctive designer without knowing it. Put yourself into the mental state of the First Knitter to achieve a "bobble" (perhaps her little kid did it while her back was turned...?). Experience: that's what the beginning handknitter is totally protected from.

The current influx of various knitting textures and colors in many of today's garments would almost certainly have staggered the handknitters of a few generations back. When I was a kid, handknitting was as plain as plain; just eternal stocking stitch, usually ornamented with ribbing here and there, and an occasional cable (which was considered VERY dashing). Just as dashing was the invention of the circular needle. I rejoice to have been born just in time for the advent of this marvellous implement. I saw my first circular needle in the knitting bag of my dear Auntie Pete on a sandy Cornish beach in 1918. Admittedly we lived in a simplified mechanical age, but in our youth somehow we felt the right to experiment and fool around with so many of the simple arts, egged on by a peculiar form of self-confidence. Is it also true that other disciplines are as bottomless as knitting? That the more you learn, the more you realize there is to know? I think so.

Elizabeth Zimmermann, Babcock, Wisconsin. June, 1989

The sub-title, *KNITTING WITHOUT A LICENSE,* may need a word of explanation to those not familiar with Elizabeth's approach to knitting, although this very approach has "caught on" with several other authors, so perhaps no explanation is required. Elizabeth's main message is that You Are The Boss Of Your Knitting. Follow your own tastes, inclinations, and instincts, and don't let yourself be intimidated into following someone else's idea of fashion. No license required. When this philosophy was first promulgated, it was regarded with suspicion, and was considered rather subversive...what? You can veer from the printed page? You can knit whatever you want? You don't have to follow orders? All you need is EPS?

Having been so close to Elizabeth all my life, it is a bit of a surprise when I occasionally step back and get a glimpse at the enormity of the effect she has had on the whole attitude towards knitting, as well as on knitting itself. At this point, her sphere of influence is so wide, that she has affected knitters who may never have even heard her name.

Since knitting has threaded itself steadily through her life, it seemed appropriate to thread her life through this knitting book. We used some sections from her original Digressions written in 1961, as explained on page 11. These have been augmented by additional opinions and anecdotes written by Elizabeth this summer.

Meg Swansen, Pittsville, Wisconsin. July, 1989

XIV

KNITTING AROUND

or

Knitting Without a License

Wearable Art Stockings

CHAPTER ONE

MOCCASIN SOCKS
and Other Stockings

Dear Knitter,

Thockies! I don't remember which of our kids had trouble enunciating "s" (perhaps all three), but I do know that anything between the shoe and the foot was called a "thockie". And so it has remained. Thus for the past four decades I've knitted no socks or stockings; just thockies. An athortment ith laid before you on the following pages.

The traditional way to knit socks is round and round on 4 (or 5) double-pointed needles, which means 8 (or 10) sharp points spreading out from the knitting hands -- slightly hedgehoggish. For those to whom this does not appeal, the new little 11.5" circular needle is a pliable and friendly tool. However, mastery of the d.p. needles is recommended, as there are situations which require their use: many knitters forego the pleasure of decreasing a circular cap down to nothing because it requires working on double-pointed needles. They would rather, when the stitches become too few to stretch around an 11.5" needle, gather the remaining stitches, bunch them all together, and, often as not, hide the resulting hole with a pom-pom. Why not give double-pointed needles a try, so you can finish off a seamless hat properly. After all, beautiful seamless garments were knitted on multiples of 6 to 8 d.p. needles long before the invention of circular needles... as exemplified by the Knitting Madonna paintings of the 1300's, depicting Mary knitting around on 4 d.p. needles.

You may work on either 4 or 5 needles (both sets are generally available), meaning you have the knitting on 4 needles and knit with the 5th; OR have the knitting on 3 needles and knit with the 4th. (It is usually mathematically easier to divide your work into quarters.)

With the knitting divided equally onto 3(4) needles and the 4(5)th needle poised to dig into the first stitch of the first needle, arrange the 3(4) needles so that the left end of Needle #1 is resting over the end of Needle #2. Now, grab the needles with your left hand so that the cross formed by Needles #1 and #2 rests in the crotch of your thumb, i.e. Needle #2 comes *under* needle #1, sticks out toward your left hand and re-appears from under your little finger. *(See photos on page 152, or the video for greater clarity.)*

Moccasin Sock in progress

To provide fortification of heels and toes (or the entire sole, as is the case with the following design), you will have to use ingenuity and imagination. The cards of Heel 'n Toe nylon you used to be able to buy in the five-and-dime are no longer being made. Inventive (and sometimes desperate) knitters have substituted strong sewing thread, embroidery floss, fish line (not too thick, or it may cut the wool from being trodden upon), and even dental floss. Some yarn companies make "sock yarn" which contains strengthening materials, and you may decide to knit the entire sock in this yarn. I still prefer to knit the sock in WOOL, and add a strand of something thin and strong to the areas which are the first to go.

The Moccasin sock design is pleasing to knit, and, because the entire sole of the foot is knitted in one piece, it can be replaced when necessary without disturbing the instep, which never seems to wear out. We call 'em RETREADS. Also, the sock itself can be knitted in a pale or pastel color, and the sole can be worked in a more practical navy or black.

Let's knit the first pair in a medium weight wool, in a medium size. Once you have grasped the principle of the design, you can vary from dress socks in Shetland wool at 6 sts to 1" to coarse outdoor socks at 4 sts to 1".

MOCCASIN SOCKS:

GAUGE: 5 stitches to 1"
SIZE: small-to-medium adult.
MATERIALS: 1 4oz skein "worsted" weight wool, 2oz contrasting color for sole, strengthening material. A set of d.p. needles and a 16" circular needle of a size to give YOU the above GAUGE (about a #4 to #6, depending upon how YOU knit).

CAST ON 44 stitches. Divide onto 3 d.p. needles (14, 16, 14) and work around in K2, P2 ribbing for wanted length to ankle (about 8" for mid-calf length).

Place 6 "heel" stitches on a piece of wool (the first and last 3 stitches of the round), and begin to work back and forth on the remaining 38 stitches as follows:

close up of toe shaping

*Right Side: Slip 1, SSK, work to antepenultimate stitch, K2 tog, K1, turn. Work back (slipping the first stitch). Repeat from * until half the original number of stitches remain (22 of them).

Now you will work back and forth on the 22 stitches (remembering to always slip the first stitch of each row) until the piece measures about 8" from the 6 stitches on a thread. (This is an arbitrary measurement; the final length of the sock will be determined by the depth of the toe knitting. Alter as you will.)

Join in strengthening thread, and change to stocking-stitch (knit on the Right side, purl back on the Wrong side). Work for about 1", or until you are about 2.5" from total wanted length of foot.

SHAPE TOE:
Divide the stitches roughly into thirds (8 stitches in the middle; 7 stitches on either side). You will now decrease as follows:

*Knit to within 1 stitch of the center section, K2 tog. Knit to last stitch of center section, SSK. Finish the row, turn, purl back. Repeat from * until the side sections have melted away, and the center 8 alone remain. (End with a knit row).

Slide the remaining 8 stitches onto the 16" circular needle, and knit up one stitch from each selvedge stitch along the lefthand side of the instep. (Since you have slipped each 1st stitch, this, in reality, will be 1 stitch for every other row. If you have insisted on knitting each 1st stitch, you will have to knit up every *other* selvedge stitch.). Knit up the 6 "heel" stitches, and the selvedge stitches down the righthand side of the instep.

You now have all stitches on the circular needle. Knit your way down the side of the instep to the 6 "heel" stitches. Now then:

HEEL SHAPING: (you may want to mark the 1st and the 6th "heel" stitches with safety pins). Knit the 6 stitches. Turn. Purl back for 7 stitches. Turn. Knit across for 8 stitches. Turn. Purl back for 9 stitches, etc, adding one more stitch at the end of each row (and always *slipping the first stitch*), until you have half the number of cast-on-stitches (22).
The heel is now shaped, and you continue with the moccasin.
Knit around on all stitches for about 1".

TOE SHAPING: Across the toe of the sock, work SSK (or K2 tog) from where the stocking-stitch begins to where it ends (about 11-13 decreases). Work for another 4-5 rounds, and repeat the toe shaping.

On this same round, work SSK decreases about 4 to 5 times across the heel stitches as well, to round it slightly. Work around a bit more.

When the entire sole is about 2" deep, you're ready to finish off as follows:
With a blunt sewing-up needle, run the wool-and-strengthening strands through the toe stitches and pull them together firmly. Put the heel stitches on a piece of wool. Divide the remaining stitches onto 2 d.p. needles (side by side), and **WEAVE** them together. Draw the heel stitches firmly together and darn in the end.

Now you see how easily you can replace (retread) the bottom of the foot when the time comes. You will simply snip a stitch in the first round, un-pick the round stitch by stitch, the sole will fall off and the selvedge stitches will be waiting to be picked up and re-knitted. At this point, you may want to try something slightly different: the Pinwheel Variation.

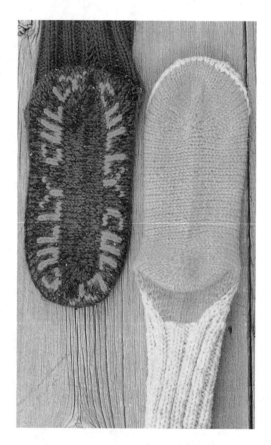

close-up of bottom of foot; "Moccasin"

4

The PINWHEEL VARIATION

PINWHEEL VARIATION:

Work around on all stitches for about 5-6 rounds. Mark 12-14 stitches centered below the heel, and begin to work back and forth on them.

*Right side: slip 1, work to last marked stitch, work it together (by SSK) with next stitch on needle. Turn. Slip 1, purl to last marked stitch and work it together (by P2 tog) with next stitch on needle. Turn.

Repeat from *, working your way up from the heel to the ball of the foot; approximately 4" from the toe.

Now put all remaining stitches on a set of d.p. needles, and work around.

PINWHEEL: Divide the stitches into 7 or 8 equal segments, and decrease 1 stitch at each segment every 2nd round. Use SSK to swirl the pinwheel to the left, or K2 tog to swirl to the right. Draw the wool through the remaining 7 or 8 stitches and finish off.

The following two socks are not shown in the video series, and are added as a bonus for you, Gentle Reader.

WOODSMAN'S THICK SOCKS

SIZES: 10-12
GAUGE: 4 stitches to 1"
MATERIALS: 2 4oz skeins 3-ply natural Sheepswool, 1oz contrasting color, if wanted. A set of d.p. needles of a size to give you the above GAUGE (about #6-7).

Starting at top, CAST ON 44 stitches. Divide onto the 3 needles with 22 stitches on 1st needle, and 11 stitches each on the 2nd and 3rd. Work in K2, P2 ribbing for about 8".

OPTION: Add a jaunty stripe of the contrasting color if wanted ... which reminds me: when changing color in ribbing, work the first round of the new color in ALL KNIT to prevent the 'wrong' side purl bloops from showing.

HEEL FLAP: Work on 1st needle only.
Row 1: Slip 1, K20, P1.
Row 2: Slip 1, K3, P14, K3, P1.
Repeat these 2 rows until heel flap measures 3", ending on the Purl side.
TO TURN HEEL:
Row 1: Slip 1, K10, SSK, K1, turn.
Row 2: Slip 1, P2, P2 tog, P1, turn.

The Woodsman's thick socks

Round 2: 1st needle: K to within last 2 stitches, K2 tog. 2nd needle: Work in ribbing. 3rd needle: SSK, K across.

Round 3: K across 1st and 3rd needles; rib across 2nd needle.

Repeat 2nd & 3rd rounds 7 times more (44 stitches). Work evenly, keeping 2nd needle in ribbing, until sock is 2.5" less than wanted length.

TO SHAPE TOE:

Round 1: 1st needle: K to last 4 stitches, K2 tog, K2. 2nd needle: K2, SSK, K to within last 4 sts, K2 tog, K2. 3rd needle: K2, SSK, K to end.

Round 2: Knit around.

Repeat rounds 1 & 2 until 20 stitches remain. Break off a length of wool and WEAVE toe stitches together.

2-color Woodsman's variation; Cross-Country stockings with shaped calf.

Row 3: Slip 1, K3, SSK, K1, turn.
Row 4: Slip 1, P4, P2 tog, P1, turn.
Row 5: Slip 1, K5, SSK, K1, turn.
Row 6: Slip 1, P6, P2 tog, P1, turn.
Row 7: Slip 1, K7, SSK, K1, turn.
Row 8: Slip 1, P8, P2 tog, P1, turn.
Row 9: Slip 1, K9, SSK, K1, turn.
Row 10: Slip 1, P10, P2 tog (12 stitches)

TO SHAPE GUSSETS:

Round 1: 1st needle (heel needle): Slip 1, K11, knit up 13 stitches along side of heel flap. 2nd needle: Rib across 2nd and 3rd needles (instep needle). 3rd needle: Knit up 13 stitches along side of heel flap and 6 stitches from 1st needle (60 sts).

WEARABLE-ART STOCKINGS

So-called because we have found no way to incorporate strengthening into the heels and toes. Thus, these stockings are for the hostess to wear, shoeless, with her feet up on the coffee-table: Socks As Art, or Sock It To Art, or Art's Socks. As Nancy Mitford said, "Americans love art so much, they even name their children it."

Two pairs of Art's Socks. Note the instep shaping, and the stitches left to be woven for the bottom of the heel.

GAUGE: 5.5 to 6 stitches to 1", depending upon whether you are knitting for spindle-shanks or tree-trunk calves.

MATERIALS: 6-8oz Main Color, 3-4oz Contrasting Color. 16" and 11.5" circular needles (or a set of d.p. needles) of a size to give you the wanted GAUGE (about size #5, give or take).

With 16" needle, in MC, **CAST ON** 60 stitches. Join and work K1, P1 for 15 rounds. Change to stocking stitch (all knit) and increase to 70 stitches in the first round (K6, M1 around).

Establish "seam" line in first 3-5 stitches and work a small repeat pattern of your choice for the "seamline" and a second pattern on the rest of the stitches. Work straight for a total of 7".

CALF SHAPING: Decrease 1 stitch each side of "seam" stitches every 4th round as follows: K2 tog, K "seam", SSK. Continue until you have 58 stitches. Work straight to ankle (about 16" total length).

FOOT SHAPING: Mark the center 3 stitches at the top of the foot (diametrically opposed to the "seam"), and increase 1 stitch each side of them *every* round by means of M1 (see drawing; you may oppose the two M1s if you wish).

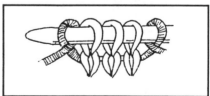

M1 , K3, M1 . On the next round, K into the back of the left M1.

7

Close up of heel stitches on a thread;
toe stitches still on the needle

The above directions are an amalgamation of the 4 or 5 pairs we knitted up. No two alike (pairs, that is), so don't feel bound to the above numbers.

Meg thinks this stocking is one of my best feats.

This top-of-foot shaping continues to the bitter end.

When the stocking is about 18" long, and you have a total of about 82-84 stitches, begin

HEEL SHAPING: Decrease 1 stitch each side of "seam" stitches *every* round: K2 tog, K "seam", SSK, for 9 rounds (consuming 18 stitches). Now place the 22 center-back sts on a thread to be woven later *(see photo above),* and continue around on about 66 stitches, still increasing at top of foot and decreasing at sole, until foot is wanted length (about 9" or so). Weave remaining toe stitches, which will make a cute pointed toe, and the stitches left on thread at heel.

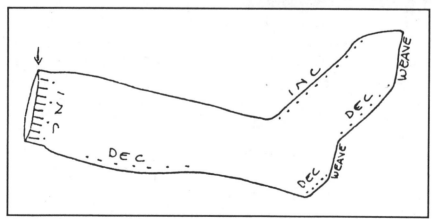

Art Sock schematic

8

The very earliest form of knitting found by archeologists was socks and stockings. Why not join this prehistoric knitting guild? If you've never yet worn woollen footwear, try it, and find out for yourself its extreme warmth and comfort. Then try knitting some for Friends and Relations.

To spur you on, I'd like to end this chapter with excerpts from a wonderful poem by a Chilean writer.

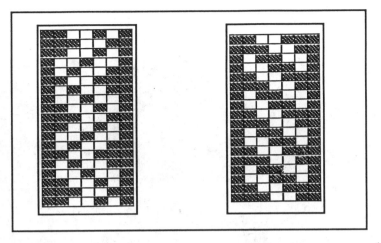

Chart for lefthand stocking on opposite page *Chart for righthand stocking on opposite page*

Note how the above patterns are mirror-imaged at the center-front and -back of the stockings.

ODE TO MY SOCKS by Pablo Neruda

Maru Mori brought me
a pair
of socks
which she knitted herself
with her sheepherder's hands,
two socks as soft
as rabbits.
I slipped my feet
into them
as though into
two cases
knitted
with threads of
twilight
and goatskin.
. . .

Nevertheless
I resisted
the sharp temptation
to save them somewhere
as schoolboys
keep
fireflies,
as learned men
collect
sacred texts,
I resisted
the mad impulse
to put them
into a golden
cage
and each day give them
birdseed
and pieces of pink melon.

. . .

The moral
of my ode is this:
beauty is twice
beauty
and what is good is doubly
good
when it is a matter of two socks
made of wool
in winter.

translated by Robert Bly

Elizabeth Zimmermann. 1964

10

DIGRESSIONS

Beginning is going to be fine and easy. Stopping will be either much less so, because of how I run on, or will be extremely easy too, because of my strong tendency, inherited no doubt from my old father, to start in a fine frenzy of enthusiasm, and then fizzle out before long. For this reason I shall limit myself to exactly one full page a day, no matter how reminiscence wells up, or how dry the well runs.

It is Friday morning, February 17th, 1961, and our last child left yesterday. This is not to say that they won't be popping in again every time the bell rings - they've been doing this ever since last summer, when Meg got through with high school - but this is the first day Arnold and I have actually been definitely, undoubtedly alone for over 23 years, and I feel it is a landmark.

For several years now I have promised myself that I will Write Things Down, but since there has been little time for this, I have made the above situation my starting point. Writing things down is, I think, going to be important for me. There are things that I remember, and things that I remember people telling me they remember, which will be gone for good when I finally die. This seems to me very sad. I wish I knew more about the people who went before me. My knowledge of the Lloyd-Joneses goes only back to a few sketchy details on my grandparents. Of the McLarens I know practically nothing at all. The maternal side is better supplied with data, both the Passmores and the Greenwoods having had the benefit of ancestry snobs during the last fifty years or so, so the basics are there.

I shall run on at length and in a surely boring fashion about the things that interest me. After all, who cares? No one has to read all this who doesn't want. I shall make a carbon for each child - and god help them if I get the paper in the wrong way - but they certainly will be no more than invited to accept the result of my tappings to take up attic space; there will be no obligation to peruse. But you never know - perhaps my grandchildren, and their children after them, will be

Betty Lloyd-Jones (Elizabeth) nearly two years old, wearing a knitted garter-stitch coat and leggings.

11

absolutely fascinated.

It is the fashion now to tremble before the bomb, and doubt that any descendants will be forthcoming, but I feel, like all fashions, this, if not absolutely to be distrusted, is still to be scrutinized with care and skepticism. Skepticism, my dear great-grandchildren, is a fine thing, and to be cultivated. Take as little on trust as you possibly can. You have quite good brains, unless my children in their time chose to ally themselves with charming morons, and you might as well practice using them. You don't have to shout your conclusions from the housetops. In my time, now, it is still possible to do this in this country, though not always wise. But so far, in no country have they found a way of knowing what you actually *think*, if you are smart enough to keep your trap shut and your eyes downcast. This is a small enough price to pay for the privilege of thinking perfectly hellish, scornful, and irreverent thoughts. And in the course of these thoughts, which are largely worthless, though satisfying, you may come upon a real pippen or two ... just look at me: a couple of nights ago I was patiently picking bobbles, or pills, off Tom's new heavy white sweater. It suddenly occured to me that Pop's haircutting electric contraption might do this faster. Suggested this to Tom, and was rewarded by Pitying Look. But I'm older now and not to be deterred so easily. I nipped upstairs for the contraption, tried it out, and it worked like a charm. Not only faster, but easier, and **much** more efficient. I immediately went to work on my beautiful plum-colored Homespun sweater, and sliced two neat holes in it through not keeping the material level. Live and learn. Then I went over the beautiful green, yellow and red skirt that my darling daughters gave me for Christmas, which has been getting a little fuzzy, with most satisfying results. Now here is the experiment, all written down. I shall probably forget it in a week or two, as I do most of my crackpot ideas, but it is Written Down, and who knows, you may benefit.

Herbert and Grace Muriel Lloyd-Jones with their firstborn, Elizabeth. 1910

So you see, my dears, use your god-given brains. They may be godgiven, but don't forget your dear old ancestors, through whose medium, partially, you received them.

Betty Lloyd-Jones. 1915

All right then. Born August 9th, 1910; first child; first grandaughter for Greenwoods; second neice for the Aunts Lloyd-Jones, and the one they saw the most of, doted on and spoiled excessively. Technically a Cockney, as born within the sound of Bow Bells in Northwick House in Maida Vale off the Edgeware Road. I can still just remember Northwick House where my parents had a ground floor flat, and were starting life very simply with only two maids ..... We must have lived there until I was 4, because I can vividly recall the outbreak of War One. There was a bevy of ladies in the drawing room, among them Auntie Pete and Auntie Carol. They were winding khaki colored wool into balls, and I was having a nest in the immense blue Chesterfield sofa with the balls of wool as my eggs. I was picked up and carried out in front of the house to watch the soldiers marching down the Edgeware Road. My father immediately enlisted in the Navy, having been in the Naval Reserve, and had to buy all new uniforms, to everybody's rage. Auntie Apay, in a very officious manner, had taken all his old uniforms, thinking he no longer needed them, and sold them as old clo', buying a wicker tea-wagon with the proceeds.

We had a summer house at Birchington in Kent, and there Mummy and the children went, while Pop was stationed for 18 months on board the HMS Agincourt in the North Sea.

"Bellair" house at Birchington, Kent. 1920

"At Scapa Flow
In early Spring;
Scapa Flow's the ve-hery thing.
Oh, you ought to see the beaches there,
The place is all ago.
We sit in the sun
And we wait for the Hun
Care of the G.P.O."

"Bellair" revisited. 1988

The Birchington house was called Bellair, after the old Lloyd-Jones house in Annerley, and we owned it until the early 1920s, so I can remember it very well. It faced North with only a field between it and the chalk cliffs, which were supposed to be dangerous as the sea was always nibbling away at them. We would pick the blossoming daffodils, narcissus and hyacinths in the spring, wrap wet cotton-wool around their stems, and send them to Pop away at Scapa Flow. Mummy would wait eagerly for Pop's letters, and type voluminous ones in reply. Then Pop was transferred to the Naval Base at Brightlingsea in Essex, and there we moved to a furnished house at 21 Church Road. It was quite a large house with a big fenced garden in the back, where Mummy immediately embarked on a kitchen garden. Some things proliferated (notably beautiful artichoke bushes, which had been there when we came, and which nobody seemed to know what to do with), and equally indigenous Greengage plum trees, yielding pot after pot of delicious jam which I can still taste on my mind's tongue.

> *"Plum Jam, Plum Jam",*
> *Said Old Dakin,*
> *"Plum Jam's the jam for me;*
> *And we shall have some 'bakin'*
> *With our plum jam for tea."*

I had a wonderful hideyhole in a gone-to-seed cabbage patch, and one day had the excitement and glory of falling through the roof of an abandoned chicken house, garnering the first permanent scar on my leg.

Betty with younger sister, Nancy,
as bridesmaids. 1916

15

CHAPTER TWO

SEAMLESS YOKE SWEATER

The original design of this garment goes back thirty-one years. It was the subject of my very first Newsletter published in 1958, and was involved in the sequence of events which drove me to produce my own publication. One of my sweater designs had been gratifyingly accepted by a yarn company (who shall remain nameless); a lovely sweater in the same colors we are using here: soft grey Shetland Wool for body and sleeves, with a blue and white Fair Isle yoke to set it off, and to embellish the portrait of the beautiful blonde who had been summoned to model it. The full page color photograph was printed on the cover, no less; a dazzling and inspiring lure to cast on Right Away. The gratification was only momentary, however. After the first wave of pride, I began checking the article, mentally following the instructions from the beginning. Well! Their instructions only *looked* as if they belonged to the sweater, and I immediately realized that old hob had been made of my original

My first cover sweater; instructions all but unrecognizable.

instructions. Misleading (to say the least) alterations had been blithely substituted for my traditional, circular, seamless sweater. Need I tell you that the directions caused the reader

16

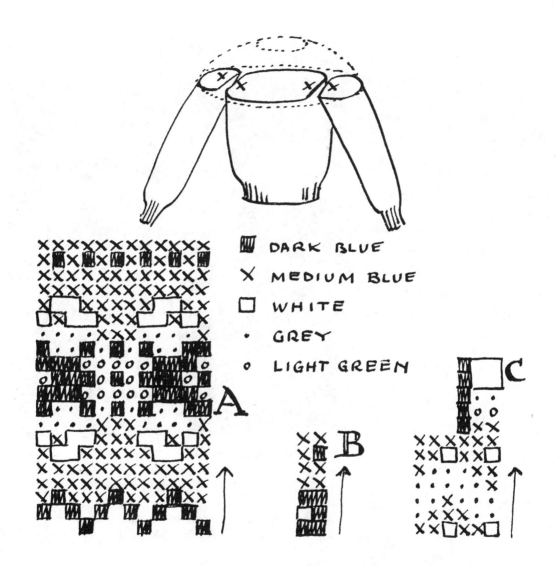

DARK BLUE

MEDIUM BLUE

WHITE

GREY

LIGHT GREEN

A

B

C

A copy of Newsletter #1 from 1958. It was titled:
Fair Isle Yoke Sweater Made Entirely On Circular Needles.

to knit a Front, a Back, two flat sleeves, and sew the pieces together...when you could plainly see in the beautious photograph that the thing had nary a seam...?

My response to the above was: "I'll do it myself said the Little Red Hen." I'll publish my own instructions. Hence: Newsletter #1. Now, 31 years later, this traditional, timeless design still looks pleasing, and I offer it to you again.

When graphing this design, I followed the two Great Rules of Fair Isle knitting: *never carry more than 2 colors on a given round,* and, *avoid a carry greater than 5 stitches long.* I also adhered to the un-spoken rules which involve color. Fair Isle knitting is unique among all other color knitting in that the background color of a given motif may change for the center one or three rounds, and the pattern color may change as well! The actual employment of color is more like painting than knitting, and the possibilities boggle the mind.

The following sweater will introduce you to E.P.S. (Elizabeth's Percentage System), a convenient and comforting method of figuring sweater proportions. As I recall, this 1958 design was the beginning of my fumbling for the mathematical formula that eventually evolved.

Elizabeth and Romper. 1925. The sweater Elizabeth is wearing in this ancient photograph was sent from Fair Isle "on appro" for her father. Years later, it was given to Gaffer, and, if you look closely at the accompanying video, you will see it held up - mends and all - when she and Meg talk about Fair Isle patterns.

As in most knitting, GAUGE is critical. The difference in my system is that I will never tell you what gauge you must get. I may tell you what materials and gauge *I* worked with, but you are encouraged to figure your own calculations based on **your own personal gauge.**

You will begin in the standard way: MAKE A SWATCH. However, since you are not heading for a dictated gauge, you will experiment with needle sizes until you achieve a knitted fabric that pleases you. Tastes vary. Some garments require a stiff, firm material (like Guernseys); others need a chicken-wire gauge (like certain lace patterns). When you have the texture that suits your project, then you are ready to take a gauge-reading; it must be exactly accurate, down to the smallest fraction of an inch. My calculator lives close by in my knitting bag.

As for the swatch itself, I am liable to make a "Swatch Cap" on a 16" circular needle, knitting the pattern I will be using in the garment. After 4-5" I will take out the needle, puff at the swatch with a steam iron, and measure from side to side (about 6-7" worth), dividing the number of stitches by the number of inches. Some knitters object that knitting a circular swatch for a circular garment is too time consuming. If 1-2 hours is too long for you, you may cast on 20-30 stitches (or several repeats of any pattern you may be using), knit across, make a long loop of wool across the back to the beginning, and knit across again. I use the loop method rather than breaking the wool at the end of each row, in case I run short of wool, and need to rip the swatch.

OK. Armed with your gauge, you are ready to begin.

Close-up of the yoke patten from Newsletter #1

SEAMLESS YOKE SWEATER

SIZE: 38" around widest part of body.
GAUGE: 6 stitches to 1"
MATERIALS: 8oz Shetland Wool in main color (silver grey), 1oz each Bressay Blue, Cornflower Blue, Cream, and Lovat Shetland Wool (see color pages). 11.5" (or a set of d.p. needles), 16" and 24" circular needles of a size to give you the above gauge. About #4-5, + 1 or 2 sizes smaller for the ribbing.

6 stitches to 1" x 38" around =

228 Key Number [K]

I want ribbing at the lower edge, and I want it to "hold in", so I will cast on 10% fewer stitches:

$$228 \times .90 = 205$$

But it has to be divisible by 4 for K2, P2 ribbing, so

CAST ON 204 stitches

onto the smaller size 24" needle.
Join, being careful not to twist, and work K2, P2 ribbing for 3-4". In the first stocking stitch round, K8, M1 around- skipping the last increase - which will get you to 228, or [K].Mark the two side "seams" by putting safety pins in stitch #1 and stitch #115. Work straight to wanted length to under-arms (15-17").

OPTION: Work short rows across the back only to prevent it from 'riding up': Knit to within 3 stitches of marked 'seam' stitch. Wrap, turn, purl back to within 3 stitches of other 'seam' stitch. Wrap, turn, continue knitting around, dealing with the wraps when you come to them. (See appendix for How To Wrap).. Repeat 1 or 2 more times, spaced a few inches apart, as you work you way up the body.

SLEEVE:

On the 11.5" (**or** a set of d.p. needles;or work back and forth and sew up the cuff seam)   **CAST ON** 20% of [K]

$$228 \times .20 = 45.6$$

which we will round off to 48 stitches (so as to be divisible by 4 for the ribbing).
K2, P2 for 4-5" for a fold-back cuff. Change to stocking stitch, and mark the 3 center underarm stitches with a safety pin. Increase 2 stitches every 5th round, i.e.
Knit to the 3 marked sts, M1, K3, M1.
Knit 4 plain rounds, and repeat. When you have increased to
    33% of [K] (76 stitches)
work straight to wanted length to underarm (about 17-18"). Knit second sleeve.

OPTION: Phoney Seams.These are good-looking, and most useful when it comes to blocking a plain sweater. You could produce them by slipping the 'seam' stitch every 2nd round - but then you would have to

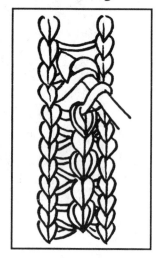

Phoney Seam. Hook up 2 stitches for every 3 rounds (ladders). Work on sides of body and underarms of sleeves

20

forego the infinite pleasure of mindlessly knitting around. In my Phoney Seam method, you make the seam all in one fell swoop when sleeves and body are finished:

DROP the marked 'seam' stitch off the needle. Cause it to drop down to the top of the ribbing (it will not 'run', but requires tugging and picking to get it down there). NOW, with a crochet hook, *hook up 2 ladders together, hook one ladder. Repeat from * all the way to the top. (see drawing on preceding page)

Phoney Seam on completed sleeve underarm. Also note the woven underarm, and the three fabrics that must unite there. More later. . .

Put 8% of [K] (which would be 18 stitches, but I will make it 17 so as to have the Phoney Seam stitch in the middle. Pure pickyness.) on threads at underarm of body and sleeves, centered directly over the "seam" stitches.

Now you are ready to UNITE the sleeves and body. Beginning where you left off on the body, knit to underarm. Drop the left end of the 24" needle, pick up the 16"

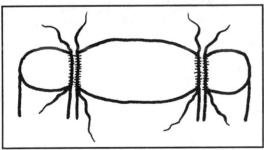

The sleeves are knitted onto the body matching the underarm stitches which are on threads.

sleeve needle, and keep on knitting around the sleeve. Abandon the 16" needle, and continue on the 24" to the other underarm. Repeat the above. You now have 134% of [K] on the needle (100% + 33% + 33% minus 4, 8%s). A relatively useless, but perhaps interesting, statistic.

Next objective:

Decrease the 134% to 40% by time the neck height is reached. There are a dozen seamless methods (so far) by which you may achieve this: Raglan, Saddle-shoulder, Shirt Yoke, Nalgar, Hybrid, Circle Yoke, Entrelac, Box-The-Compass, Set-in-Sleeve, Bohus, Lap-shoulder, and Yoke. I think the yoke method is the easiest and most versatile, allowing for a variety of color or texture patterns to be inserted between the decrease rounds.

21

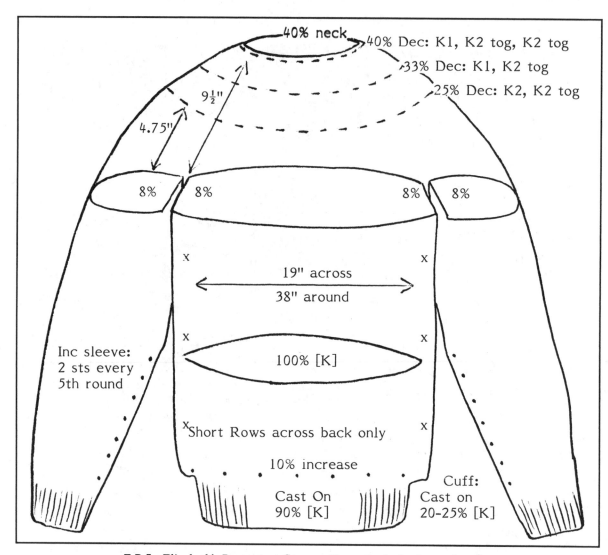

E.P.S.: Elizabeth's Percentage System. Here are the basic numbers for both stitch count and measurement.

Another interesting discovery I've made over the years, as I tried to get a handle on how deep the yoke should be, is in *measurement* rather than percentages:

The DEPTH of the yoke is approximately HALF the WIDTH of the body. Again - there is a lot of leeway here, but this will give you a starting point. AND: in a yoke sweater, the first decrease round is not worked until HALF the yoke depth has been knitted. Imagine.

So: if the body is 38" around, it is 19" across, and the yoke depth will be about 9.5". There will be three decrease rounds, but the first will not be worked until about 4.75" worth of plain knitting have been achieved.

I said *plain knitting* as that is my preference. I like a fairly shallow yoke pattern, but feel free to insert an additional design of your choice before the first yoke decrease.

22

After 4.75" of plain knitting around, it is time for the **FIRST DECREASE:** Beginning behind left shoulder (for pullover); or at center front (for Henley Neck):

K2, K2 together, around
(A decrease of 25%; you are turning 4 stitches into 3.)
Work PATTERN A.

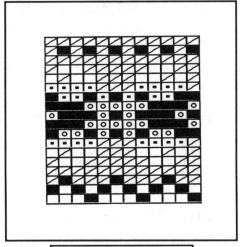

= DARK BLUE
= TARTAN BLUE
= CREAM
= GREY
= LOVAT

Work **SECOND DECREASE:**
K1, K2 together, around
(A decrease of 33.3%; you are turning 3 stitches into 2.)
Work PATTERNS B and C

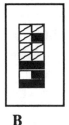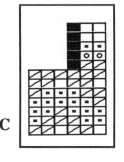

B   C

Work **THIRD DECREASE:**
K1, K2 tog, K2 tog, around
(A decrease of 40%; you are turning 5 stitches into 3.)

The number of stitches now on your needle should be about 40% of [K] (93).

FUDGING:
This is permitted, yea, even encouraged and necessary in knitting. When I began the 12-stitch repeat pattern, it did not fit evenly into the stitches on my needle; I had a fudge factor which required a sneaky increase of 4 sts. I made 1 stitch in each quarter of the plain round preceding the pattern...OR, I could have eliminated 4 of the decreases if I had anticipated earlier on.

HOWEVER, if you are knitting the Henley Neck version, the pattern need not fit in evenly. You will begin your pattern round at the center front, carefully balancing the leftover stitches of the pattern on either side. Be most particular about this, as it is the focal point of the sweater.

OK, we're now ready to insert **SHORT ROWS** across the back of the neck. This is very necessary to the proper fit of the garment.

Mark the 2 shoulder points with safety pins. Knit (in background color) to within 3-4 stitches of the left pin: Wrap, turn, purl back to within 3-4 stitches of the other pin. Wrap, turn, knit to - and deal with - first wrap. Knit 3 more stitches. Wrap, turn, purl back to - and deal with - purl wrap. Purl 3 more stitches. Wrap, turn, Knit back. Continue for a total of 3 sets of Short

Rows (6 extra rows)

OPTIONS: Some knitters object to having additional plain knitting above the color-pattern on the back. If you are one of those knitters, you have two other choices.

1. You may insert the short rows in the main body of the yoke <u>before</u> you begin the color pattern.

2. You may insert the short rows in the ribbing around the neck, or in the garter-stitch trim of the Henley Neck.

NECK BORDER:
Work around on all neck stitches in K2, P2 ribbing for about 1.5- 2"(or wanted height). Cast Off very loosely (so neck will fit over a human head). If the neck is too sloppy, skim elastic thread through the inside.

WEAVING UNDERARMS:
This is the final detail that makes the sweater truly Seamless. We still see directions telling knitters to *cast off* the underarm stitches and sew them together, but how unattractive as well as uncomfortable for the wearer. Weaving is such a satisfying skill to have. Quite magical, to boot.

Transfer the stitches from their threads to a pair of d.p. needles.

NOW:
Pick up an additional "stitch" from each corner as follows: pick up a running thread from the fabric, twist it into a stitch and put it on the needle. This is important in helping to avoid a hole at each corner. After all, the knitting is coming from three different directions, all converging at that corner *(see photo)*, and it needs help. So, if you had 17 stitches on a thread, you will be weaving 19 stitches. WEAVE. *(see appendix)* There is still liable to be a slight hole, so work a kind of duplicate stitch around the loose areas, and snug them up.

DARNING IN ENDS:
This requires time and patience, but, when skillfully done, you can all but eliminate the "jog" at the beginning of the rounds.I hope you have resisted the temptation to carry an unused wool up beyond 2-3 rounds, so you will have a great many ends to darn in. Take hold of one end. Looking at the right side of the garment, tug the end up, down, and sideways...which way should it go to align itself with its neighbor? Skim it through the wrong side with a sharp needle.

CHILD'S YOKE SWEATER
This is the same concept as an adult's circular sweater: knitted from the bottom up, seamless, decreased at the yoke by 3 rounds of regular decreases, and shaped at the neck back by 6 short rows. Decide on the width you want for the body, multiply the inches by your gauge and find your Key Number [K]. Cast on 90% of [K] for ribbing. Increase to 100% in first stocking stitch round, and work to underarm.

Make the body as long as you can bear, to allow for growth.

I like straight sleeves, the better to fit a child's straight arms. I usually cast on 20- 25% of [K], rib like mad, and increase severly in the first plain round to 40%.

Henley-neck Yoke Sweater

Long Cuffs of ribbing are mandatory - their purpose being to adapt for as long as possible to those astonishingly growing arms. In the larger sizes you may like to shape the lower sleeves slightly. Sleeves should have about 40% of [K] at the top.

When body and sleeves are the wanted length, put 8% of [K] on pieces of wool at underarms on body and sleeves. UNITE all remaining stitches on the 24" needle, and tear into the yoke.

The yoke differs from that on an adult size, as children's heads are proportionately larger, so the neck-opening is 50% of [K] instead of 40% for an adult sweater. The disconcerting fact that the child's neck is proportionately *smaller* is taken care of by a few rounds of elastic

thread skimmed through the top of the inside of the neck ribbing. Thus it will pass easily over the head, and still fit the neck neatly.

The decrease rate for the yoke gave me first headaches, then gratified amazement, and lastly a strong feeling of awe. We need 50% at the neck, and the percentages have been gummed up by the relatively wide sleeves. I must have bescribbled large areas with my empirical arithmetic; this is the surprisingly simple result:

1st DEC: K2, K2 tog around (1/4)
2nd DEC: K1, K2 tog around (1/3)
3rd DEC: K1, K2 tog around (1/3)

The yoke measurements mirror the adult version: the depth of the yoke is half the body width; the first decrease is worked after half the yoke has been knitted.

25

THE HENLEY NECK VARIATION

You may convert a pullover into a Henley Neck after the fact, but it is a bit simpler if you have made up your mind by time you begin the color-pattern.

Mark the center 3-5 stitches. Keep them in background color as you work the pattern, anchoring the carried color in the center stitch every now and then. (This will act as a built-in basting thread for the cutting to come.)

Continue around as for crew neck sweater. When the pattern has been completed, put all neck stitches on a thread.

With a small stitch and loose tension, machine stitch down the front, across the bottom, and up the other side of the basting, staying fairly close to the center stitch. If you feel nervous, run a second row of machine stitching next to the first. Cut on the basting. Beginning at bottom of the cut, with smaller needle, Knit Up 2 stitches for every 3 rounds up the side; knit up all neck stitches, and 2 for 3 down the other side.

Work back and forth in garter-stitch, inserting a few short rows across the back of the neck if not already incorporated in the body, and mitering the corners as follows:

Mark the top corner stitch. Work an increase each side of the marked stitch every 2nd row. Keep the marked stitch in knit by purling it on the wrong side to produce a snappy diagonal line at the corner (see photo)

After 3 ridges, work small, evenly-spaced buttonholes by YO, K2 tog. Work 3 more ridges, and cast off: I like to use **Sewn Casting Off** on garter-stitch. *(see appendix)*. Tack down the lower edges of each border. Neaten cut edges *(see page 172)*. Sew on buttons. There.

C.

B.

A.

Chart for the Henley Neck yoke shown on page 25, and in the color section.

Using Silver Grey as a Main Color, here are three choices for color combinations:		
o = Strawberry	Cornflower	Ghillie Green
x = Lavender	Bressay Blue	Green Lovat
• = Framboise	Periwinkle	Lovat
''' = Burgundy	Navy blue	Loch Maree
/ = Cream	Cream	Cream
2 = Knit 2 tog	Knit 2 tog	Knit 2 tog

... Digressions

By 1917 a few Zeppelins had been spotted close to where we lived, and since a new baby was expected anyway, it seemed a good idea to unload me onto the Aunts in Stretham for a bit. Off I went to spend a wonderful winter being spoiled by father's four sisters: Gert, Lloie, Offie and Apay. They lived at 21 Mount Nod Road in a real Victorian house with coloured glass in the front door, a striped awning to protect it from the sun, a monkey tree in front of the house, and a circular drive up which no one drove. Inside was the drawing-room, with wonderful draped curtains and curved glass cupboards containing curios, among them an ostrich egg with a bird painted on it. Across the large hall was the morning-room, and the spacious dining-room with a door leading onto the verandah. I can't remember ever doing much living or sitting in any of these rooms, but think this must have been be-

Elizabeth, her mother Grace Muriel and Nancy. 1915

cause the Aunts were always busying themselves with something, even if it was only washing the best china, or polishing the umbrella handles, or even taking little naps. They had two servants, but were very exacting housekeepers, and kept busy all day except for actual teatime which was usually in the morning room. I had a "nursery" on the half landing (where there was also a bathroom with the tub set into a mahogany frame), and a room to myself over the front portico, which had been my father's room, and where the blue persian cat, Michael, used to perch himself on my bed in a very comforting fashion.

All four sisters had doted on my father, who was the youngest, and it was almost a foregone conclusion that they would not look favourably on any wife he might choose. Therefore the relationship between the grownups above me was fairly strained, although I became conscious of this only by very slow and instinctive degrees, as neither Lloyd-Joneses nor Greenwoods ever once perpetrated anything so vulgar as a quarrel. Nor did they ever lose their tempers with us children, although

they were experts at being disappointed, or ashamed of us, or having hurt feelings. So although we were often magnanimously forgiven for things, we never experienced the pleasure of a fight followed by a lovely tearful emotional reconciliation.

Anyway the Aunts made an enormous fuss of me, and Mummy says she can distinctly remember seeing me absorbed in a book with the devoted Auntie Lloie lacing up my boots to go to school. I walked to school of course, with a bevy of local kids who gradually picked each other up on the way there. They didn't like me much and teased me and made me feel quite unhappy. But then I was so puffed up with myself from being praised and admired at home that I must have been an unbearable child.

Elizabeth's father, Herbert Lloyd-Jones, and Romper.

I loved Miss Pearce's School, and was absorbed happily into the first form, where I meticulously back-stitched a child's blouse; then into the second form where I was set to work hemming a pink pinafore.

Auntie Gert was The Musical One, and gave me my first piano lessons, which were excellent ones. Auntie Lloie was the Artistic One, and gave me lessons in oil painting. Auntie Offie was the Housekeeping One, and taught me to sew; in fact, she took a special course in How To Teach One's Little Niece To Make Doodads Out Of Matchboxes and Glue... Auntie Apay was The Invalid; most families in those days contained one of these. She was the youngest (except for Pop) and had had the distinction of having spent some time in Paris as a girl. She was therefore the expert on all things French: language, accent, fashion, etc, which impressed me. She had had some kind of a stroke, and her whole left side was semi-paralyzed. She could get around all right, but her face was slightly lop-sided, and she must have suffered considerable discomfort. Since this had happened when she was about 17, it was of course a great misfortune, and Offie had decided to devote herself to this afflicted sister, and deny herself all thoughts of marriage. There was a family story to the effect that somebody had wanted to marry Offie very badly, and never married anybody else, and used to write to her every birthday for years. The two elder sisters, Lloie and Gert, did not marry either. They all four always said that "they decided as a family not to marry" which sentiment Mummy despised and made mock of. After all they had seen their beloved elder sister, Dora, die in childbirth, and didn't think much of their brother's wife or family life. Perhaps old Thomas Lloyd-Jones had been such a tyrant when alive that he scared off all suitors. Anyway, they did not marry, but divided themselves into two pairs: Lloie and Gertrude, and Offie and Apay, and lived together for the rest of their lives.

Uncle Benny, his Rolls, Aunt Kate and Uncle Paul, visiting Arnold and Elizabeth in Starnberger See. 1934

29

What follows is all I can remember having been told about my great-grandparents McLaren, and is really the heart of the matter, because this is the kind of detail that when it is lost is gone forever. My memory of course is faulty; I must have been told this by one of the Aunts when I was a youngish child, and not paying too much attention anyway.

Great-grandmother McLaren was ailing - tuberculosis - and a sea voyage was prescribed, so I suppose great-grandfather decided to combine the well known therapy of that time with emigration. That was about 1850, and they plumped for South Africa, setting off in a sailing ship with all their children. Great-grandmother did not survive the voyage, and was buried at sea. Thus her husband and small children landed in the new raw colony with a bleak prospect indeed. Annie, my grandmother, was only eight years

Elizabeth and her father.

old, and had I don't know how many younger brothers and sisters. They lived in a tent. And this is all I know. I don't think the young husband married again, because Annie brought up the younger children, for some years anyway, and I've never heard of any stepmother. When Annie was eighteen, Thomas Lloyd-Jones appeared on the scene, a young emigrating Welshman from Ruthin (pronounced "rithin") in North Wales. He was twenty-five, and rumour has it that he didn't learn to speak English until he was grown up. He and Annie were married, lived in Durban, and soon produced a fair-sized family of girls: Dora, Annie (Lloie), Gertrude, Florence (Offie) and Ada Crawford (Apay). It was not until they returned to England, and were living in Kensington, that my father, Herbert, was born in 1877. And that brought the family to a close.

Annie must have been a good mother and a clever one. I can still remember the charming little kimonos which she ran up on the machine for the girls when they were "three little maids from school" in the Mikado. All the children were devoted to her. She had a round face, dark eyebrows, I believe blue eyes, and slightly crimpy hair parted in the middle. This is taken from an enlarged photograph which hung over my parents' bed. The counterpart of Thomas shows a very different aspect - a real old tyrant, I should say. Heavy black black eyebrows, dark piercing eyes, and a splendid pointed beard. The family liked to believe that he had a touch of Spanish blood, dropped in Wales after the Armada, when the Spanish fleet tried to escape up the Channel and around the British Isles, many of them being wrecked

on the savage and rocky West coast. I don't know what Thomas did for a living;
"Something in the city", I suppose. He still kept ties with South Africa. My Pop used
to say he was sure he had something to do with the slave trade, although this may
of course be put down to Pop's love of saying upsetting things. For instance, that he
had an uncle in a loony-bin, or that an ancestor of his had been in the Battle of
Waterloo, and had been famous for running away from it.

One day my grandfather set off for South Africa on a business trip. He bade
goodbye to his family at home, and would be gone for several months. That evening
as they were sitting around the supper table -- feeling, I imagine, very relaxed, and
probably feasting on some delicious dish that Father disapproved of -- a voice
behind them intoned, "Jimmy, put that picture straight." Tableau! He hadn't gone
after all, and this became a famous family saying and anecdote. He was always very
fussy about straight pictures, and so was my father after him. They hardly bother
me at all. "Jimmy" was his pet name for his second child, Annie. He must have
wanted a boy very badly indeed, and had the name Lloyd picked out for him. When
Annie was born, he used to call her "Lloydie", which became changed to Lloie, and
survives today in our own Lloie.

Nancy, Pringle and Elizabeth. 1920

31

In March of 1918, my parents' third and final daughter was born when Nancy and I were five and seven. My nose was now quite definitely out of joint, as Nancy was the blonde, charming one and Pringle was the baby; I was just the clever one, and as there was no other emotional outlet for me, I expressed myself in savage fights with my sister, Nancy. Mummy *would* adjudicate our squabbles, and I maintain that this is impossible to do, as what grown-up can possibly be versed in all the hidden tensions and reasons for children's spats? Also, the attention given to these small outbursts of momentary childish anger magnifies them enormously, and makes the child important, so that it turns again and again to this form of atten-

Nancy and Elizabeth. 1917

tion-getting, until it begins to hate its sibling. I really hated my sister, Nancy, or at least was convinced that I hated her. I was also convinced that I loved my mother. So you can see what a tangle I was in. Nancy was an epileptic, and not much was known in those days about what was considered a fairly shameful affliction. Nancy died when she was 15 and I was 17, just starting my pensionnat year in Switzerland, and my guilt feeling at not having loved her was quite overwhelming.

*Elizabeth's pencil sketch of Meg, reluctantly holding
a skein . New Hope, PA. 1947*

CHAPTER THREE

FIVE KNITTED DICKEYS
&
A VERY WARM HAT

We call 'em Dickeys. They go around the human neck in parky weather and keep it snug and secure. Since they must first pass over the human head, the more stretchable they are, the better. In fact, they should (and even must) be knitted; why else would I be telling you about them?

Dickey von Beethoven

Consider the circumference of the human head and neck; the Dickey must be obliging enough to stretch comfortably over the actual head, yet snuggle down around the neck of the victim when the time comes. Let us bless the elasticity of handknitting, and cast on sufficient stitches to fit either circumference equally well - neither too tight, nor, god save us, too sloppy.

Not only do they warm and protect your neck and upper chest, but, worn under a turned up shirt collar, they look very sporting indeed.

Three versions of the Dickey Simple. If you want to add a jaunty stripe, work the first round of the new color in All Knit (see chapter 1) to prevent a "wrong side" appearance.

A Dickey is a good beginning-knitter's project, so let's start with one in thickish wool, involving a few interesting details.

DICKEY SIMPLE

MATERIALS: 1 4oz skein 2-ply Sheepswool, Homespun or Fisherman. (These are "our" wools; naturally you may use any medium-weight wool that will yield the required gauge.) A 16" circular needle, approximately #5-6.
GAUGE: 5 stitches to 1" measured over stocking-stitch.

CAST ON 76 stitches. K2, P2 for 2" for a stand-up collar, or 4-5" for a fold-over turtleneck.
CAST OFF 18 stitches across the back, and you will now work back and forth as follows:
Right Side: Slip 1, SSK *(see appendix)*, rib to the last 3 stitches, K2 tog, P1. Turn.
Wrong Side: Slip 1, rib to last stitch, P1.

Repeat these 2 rows until 26 stitches remain (or wanted width). Continue straight for another 2-3" (or wanted length). **Cast Off.** Simple, huh?

DICKEY SIMPLER

Cast On 96. Rib to wanted neck depth. Cast Off back 48, and rib back and forth on front 48 to wanted length. Cast Off. Simpler, huh?

Dickey and Mikey

If you have never Turned a Corner in garter-stitch before, make this little swatch before launching into the next design:

CAST ON 10 stitches.
K9, turn, knit back.
K8, turn, knit back.
K7, turn, knit back....etc.
until you get to
K2, turn, knit back. **NOW:**
K3, turn, knit back.
K4, turn, knit back....etc.
back up to K10.
Corner turned.

DICKEY von BEETHOVEN
(in all garter-stitch)

MATERIALS: 2oz Shetland Wool. Needle size #3 or 4; either a 16" circular, or a pair of straight needles.
GAUGE: 6 stitches to 1 inch.
CAST ON, using Invisible Casting On, *(see appendix)* 40 stitches: 20 for the neck, and 20 for the Surround. Work back and forth in garter-stitch for 14 Ridges or 28 rows (2 rows equal 1 garter-stitch ridge).
Turn First Corner (see above) on the 20 Surround stitches, leaving the 20 neck stitches on the needle - ignored. When you get down to "K7, turn, knit back", reverse matters and begin to turn the corner back up to 20 stitches.

37

Knit 12 Ridges on all 40 stitches for the side of the neck. **Turn Second Corner** over the 20 Surround stitches, down to only 2 stitches this time.

As you begin turning the second corner back up again, **increase** 1 stitch at the selvedge edge of each row. By the time you have turned the full corner, you should have a total of 60 stitches (20 for the neck and 40 for the Surround).

Work 20 Ridges (40 rows) for the front. NOW, reverse the foregoing: **Turn Third Corner**, and **decrease** 1 stitch at the selvedge edge of each row down to 2 stitches; turn second-half of corner back to 40 stitches total. Knit 12 Ridges. **Turn Fourth Corner**. Work a final 14 ridges, remove the auxiliary thread from the Invisible casting on, and **weave** *(see appendix)* the end to the beginning. Run a few rounds of elastic thread through the inside of the neck, as garter-stitch tends to stretch.

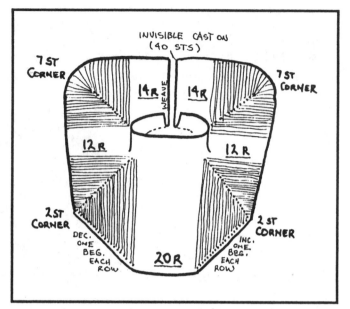

BEETHOVEN'S VARIATIONS ON A DICKEY
(see photo below)

On a 16" circular needle (#3 or 4), in Shetland Wool, at a **gauge** of 6 stitches to 1", **CAST ON** 96 stitches. Work around in K2, P2 ribbing for about 3" (or wanted neck depth). Do not cast off.

At center back, Invisibly CAST ON 18 stitches, and begin working back and forth in garter-stitch. You will be working perpendicularly to the ribbed neck, and will unite the Surround to the neck by knitting the last stitch of each ridge **together** with a waiting neck stitch. Choose K2 tog, *or* SSK, *or* Slip 1, K1, psso, *or* K2 tog tbl (through back loops). *(see appendix)*

Work 19 ridges. Turn 1st corner (see p 37). Work 16 Ridges for side of neck. Turn

38

2nd corner (increasing for front section - as above). Work 26 Ridges for front section. Turn 3rd corner (decreasing as above). K 16 Ridges for neck side. Turn 4th corner. K 19 Ridges, and weave end to beginning.

CORRUGATED DICKEY

WARNING: Corrugated Ribbing consists of K2 stitches in one color, then P2 stitches in a second color. It has no elasticity, so prepare to rip your ears off pulling it on, and snub your nose tearing it off; but it is good looking, and has a pleasing stability.

MATERIALS: 1 oz assorted colors of Shetland Wool. A 16" circular needle, about size #3 or 4.
GAUGE: 6 stitches to 1".
CAST ON 100 stitches. K2, P2 in two colors. After 2", change to one-color ribbing, and increase 50% across the back 46 stitches as follows:
*K1, M1, K1. P1, M1, P1. Repeat from * across back 46 stitches only.
Continue around, remembering to work K3, P3 across the back, and K2, P2 on the front 54 stitches.
After 1", CAST OFF the back stitches, and

work back and forth on the front 54 for another 5". At 1" from wanted length, decrease one stitch at the beginning and end of the last 3-4 rows to keep the corners from flaring out. Cast off.

TRICKY DICKEY

MATERIALS: 2 oz Shetland Wool. 16" circular needle, about #3 or 4.
GAUGE: 6 stitches to 1".
CAST ON 96 stitches. K2, P2 for 3", or wanted neck height.

OPTION: Insert a stripe or two in the neck section. If you do not want a 'wrong side' appearance to your ribbing, work the first round of a new color in all knit.

Put 54 stitches on a thread at center back. Work back and forth on front 42 stitches

39

only (still working in K2, P2 ribbing) for 3.5"

OPTION: For a nice braided selvedge: slip the first stitch and purl the last stitch of each row.

Next: Decrease 1 stitch at the beginning and end of each Right-side row as follows:
Right Side: Slip 1, SSK, rib to within 3 stitches of end, K2 tog, P1. Turn.
Wrong Side: Slip 1, rib to last stitch, P1. Repeat these two rows until you have 26 stitches.
Do not cast off.
TRIM: Knit up stitches from along the selvedge of the piece you just completed: 1 stitch for each selvedge stitch - which, if you have slipped each first stitch, will be

Tricky Dickey. Stripes are optional.

half the number of rows. Work across the back stitches that were left on a thread - and, as you go, **increase** 50% as follows: K1, M1, K1. P1, M1, P1. In other words, you will increase 1 stitch into each K2 and P2 section. This increase will flare out the neck-back, and help keep the Dickey in place.
Knit up the stitches down the other front selvedge, and work around on all stitches for an inch or so - remembering to K3, P3 across the neck back stitches.
Cast off.

Arnold and Eizabeth wearing Dickeys

OPTION: For a deeper trim around the back of the neck, work another increase across the neck back after 1-1.5". Also, for a superior fit on any of the preceding models, work a short row across the back of the vertical neck section.

Pencil sketch: "The Kidners. 1948"

Blow, thou winter wind! My DICKEY protecteth me.

VERY WARM HAT
(Reversible)

MATERIALS: 4 oz medium weight wool; use 2-ply Icelandic for super warmth. A 16" circular needle and a set of double pointed needles, approximately #5-6. Oddments of wool for color patterns (optional).

GAUGE: 5 stitches to 1". (If worked at a gauge of 4 stitches to 1", cast on 20% fewer stitches.)

CAST ON 91 stitches.

OPTION: If you want to knit in the pattern chart shown here, CAST ON 92 stitches to fit the 4-stitch repeat pattern evenly. Get rid of the extra stitch near the top of the hat - at the beginning of the decrease rounds.

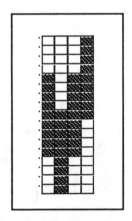

The Very Warm Hat. Tuck one into the other, and the hat becomes double-thick and reversible.

Join, being careful not to twist, and knit around for 6-8" (or more), adding whatever color or texture patterns strike your fancy.

OPTION: A word about casting on: if you use "long-tail" casting on, and consider the outline stitch side to be the right side, you may then knit up into the purl bumps behind the outline stitch when you come to knit the second hat. If you choose a different cast on, then PURL the very first round to facilitate the fold between the two hats.

42

to K2 tog at the mid-point. *You may also decrease in a straight vertical line by means of a double-decrease worked every 4th round. If you work the 7 decreases less frequently, the hat will be pointed; speed them up, and you have a pillbox top.*

SHAPE TOP: Make sure you have 91 stitches, and decrease 7 stitches evenly spaced around as follows: K11, K2 tog. K 1 round plain. Repeat these two rounds (the "K11" will become K10 K2 tog, K9 K2 tog, K8 K2 tog, etc.) until there are 49 stitches left. Change to double-pointed needles and decrease EVERY round until there are 7 stitches left. Finish off by running the working wool through the 7, pulling firmly to close the top, and darning it in.

LINING: In a contrasting color, knit up 91 (or 92) stitches from around the cast on edge, and repeat the above.

These instructions are for a conventional shape. Follow these for your first hat; then go careening off in your own idiosyncratic direction for all subsequent hats; no two alike.

OPTION: The top shaping leaves the door wide open for experimentation. Do you want your hat to be flat-topped? Pointed? Spiralled? Knitter's choice.
K2 tog will cause the decrease line to swirl to the right. You may choose SSK instead and veer to the left. Or, how about a zig-zag: begin with SSK and switch

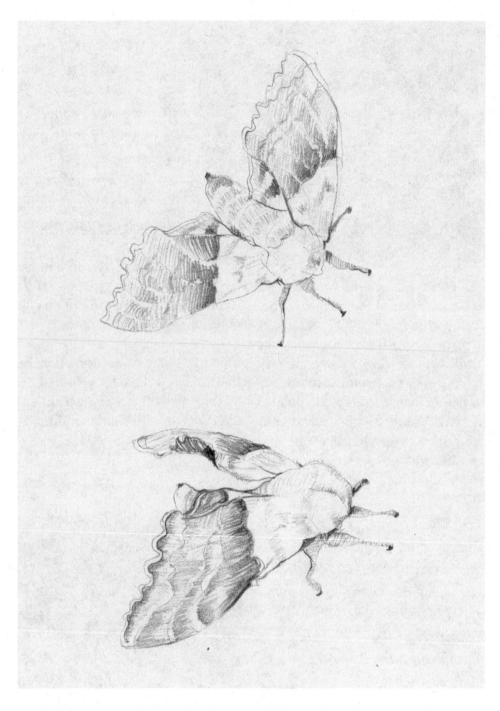

Elizabeth's pencil drawing of a Poplar Sphynx moth
as a gift for son Thomas. June, 1971.
(not *a wool m--h)*

. . . Digressions

In the early summer of 1918 there was a general feeling that the war couldn't last much longer, and Auntie Pete suggested to Mummy that she take the whole gang and spend the summer at Polzeath in Cornwall. She said it was a beautiful, unspoiled place where the children could run wild. Good Auntie Pete.

This summer in Polzeath was to be the halcyon memory of my entire childhood and youth. When it was over I used to cry myself to sleep whenever something had upset me, longing to go back to it. We moved there lock, stock and barrel, with two maids, and rented an entire house on the left side of the bay, which is today a boarding house. It was an old stone building with only a narrow, walled path between it and the actual cliffs going down sheer into the sea at high tide. It and Miss Maberly's Shop were the only things on that thrift- and gorse-clad side of the bay, but on the North side was what we called Clacton: a row of boarding-

Auntie Pete, her donkey Merrilegs, and Elizabeth
Circa 1912

houses occupied by families who had discovered Polzeath and came there year after year with their children. There was also a hotel where the Vanbrugh sisters (Violet and Irene ... actresses ...) stayed, and shed an aura of fame.

I attended Mr. Rosevear's little summer school of a dozen or so kids, held mornings in Mr. Rosevear's dining-room. I can only remember reading in its entirety a large book and a dull one, called *Denizens of the Jungle*, and I never did quite grasp what denizens were; I thought it was that they lived in dens, and I somehow confused them with the Scarlet Pimpernel on account of there being a z in Orczy. The school was at Trebetherick, where was also Saint Enedoc's Church with the crooked steeple, and I used to walk over every morning.

I was seven going on eight, was just starting to read, and was already experimenting with knitting which was to be such a prop and comfort in my middle and old age. And, thanks to Mummy's good sense, I was allowed to run completely wild.

Nancy and I had green teazle-wool sweaters, with yellow squares on them, and played all day on the sands, in the rocks, in the caves, and climbing sure-footedly on scarifying cliffs. Mummy held, quite rightly, that it is a major sin to implant fear in a child's mind. Let it be fearless, and caution will come of itself. But fear gives unsureness, and this unbalances. You can't possibly watch a child every minute of its life, so the least you can do is to give it confidence in itself to protect it when you are not there.

Elizabeth's ink sketch of rooftop view. Mons, Belgium. 1970

Betty and Nancy

One of my earliest memories has always been of a day when I pestered my mother to teach me how to knit. The female half of my mother's family knitted uninterruptably, and they rather scorned the females of my father's family who knitted exclusively mats and potholders.

"Well," said my mother, "If you're good all day today, I'll teach you tomorrow."

A woman of her word she was, so I was GOOD .. all day. The next day, Mummy was sitting in the dining-room, knitting around. I can see that sweater (jersey to us, of course) to this day. It was bright green, in stocking-stitch, on four needles (no circulars in those days), and destined for me myself. So I perched on her lap and she put her knitting in front of me.

" Take a needle in each hand," she said, "and put the righthand needle into the first stitch on the lefthand needle. Now pick up the wool with your right hand, and loop it round the righthand needle, from back to front. Then hoick it through the other stitch, the one on the lefthand needle, slipping this stitch off."

This was repeated several times, to the poetic remark of " slip, over, under, off."

"See?" she said. "One stitch knitted! Let's do it again."

So we did. And then a third time.

" That's enough for today," she said.

Such excitement. She must have taught me to purl sometime too, but of this I have no recollection except that it was a bit awkward to achieve.

I took that sweater with me and wore it when we all went for that summer in Polzeath; all except my father, who was in a battleship in the North Sea. When Auntie Pete came to visit us there, I proudly showed her my knitting. She extinguished my pride immediately by showing me her knitting: four of the skinniest little double-pointed needles, deeply involved in a circular piece of knitting about

Elizabeth's father Herbert Lloyd-Jones (center) on duty during WWI.

three inches long. It was to be a sock.

"Show me!"

So she did. Off I went, on to the cliffs, to knit, and had the time of my life. I soon discovered that I was working a bit loosely, so tightened up a bit, especially when moving from one needle to the next.

Later that day, Auntie Pete demanded her knitting back, so as to be able to get on with it herself, and gently commented on its looseness where one needle had joined another. I was cut to the quick, but said nothing, possibly having instinctively realized My Life Was Starting. When she ripped my few rows, my little heart almost broke. But I'd learned HOW TO KNIT, and have never stopped since.

The Greenwood family consisted of a bunch of excellent knitters. My Auntie Carol even contributed sweater designs to *Walson's Magazine* , and of course they all "threw their wool" with the right hand, which I did too.

We stayed in Polzeath for three whole months, and I shall never forget it, although I have of course long since ceased to mourn it. I don't mourn any place any more; all that is left is nostalgia. I know now that there were many beautiful places still ahead of me. But when we left that Southerly shore of Cornwall and came back to Birchington to live, I didn't know this.

Before that, there was a short interlude for Nancy and me staying with the Aunts on a farm in Devonshire. I have forgotten the name of the place, but it was our first

Baby Betty at the shore

48

experience on a real farm, with an actual RIVER. Really it was a small brook, but it had an island completely surrounded by running water, and for a child accustomed only to the salty back-and-forth rhythm of the sea, this was sheer magic.

In the Autumn of 1918, my father was gradually demobilized, and we all moved to Bellair in Birchington, Kent, with Lizzie, the cook from Norfolk, her sister Elsie (Nanny Tibble had married the Birchington fishmonger) and a Swiss girl, Hélène Forney from Lausanne, to look after baby Pringle. There were also two fine tabby cats, Muckle Flugga and Scrabster (place names from the North of Scotland where Pop had been stationed in the *Agincourt*). I went to Miss Barnes's School, in the village, but pretty soon it was decided that it would be better to try a governess for a change, so Miss Barrett arrived.

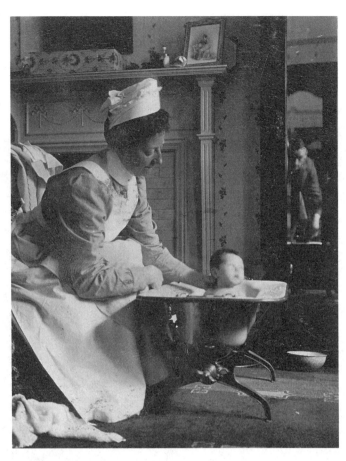

Baby Elizabeth with Nanny having her bath. 1910

Ah Miss Barrett. Poor thing, she suffered terribly from rheumatism and had a pitiful limp. What worse place for her to have to live than this draughty and wind-swept bungalow-with-rooms-in-the-roof right on the North Sea. This was the height of the fad for Fresh Air, and I remember the bedroom curtains flapping against the ceiling all night and burrowing right under the bedclothes, head and all, in search of a little warmth. Poor Miss Barrett. We memorized the list of what was necessary to keep her warm in bed: woolly vest, flannel nightgown, bedsocks, bedjacket and woolly nightcap, two hot water bottles, and piles of eiderdown quilts. She took us for endless windy walks about the dull, flat countryside, and only rarely where we loved to go, along the beach. Especially on windy days the beach yielded fine pieces of driftwood for the fire, which was an improvement on the peat squares which my parents used.

49

One morning, there, in front of the gas-stove sat the Swiss Governess Hélene, a long blue stocking for the baby-sister hanging from four regular knitting needles - - but what was **that**? The stocking was slowly growing, but the hands weren't knitting; the right hand hooked the stitches through all right, but around the **left** forefinger was looped the wool itself.

"Montrez moi," I said. And she did. I was fascinated, and I immediately set to practising this new, and obviously more efficient way of knitting.

Before long, Miss Barrett made her entrance, poised for the morning's lessons.

She took one look at me and said, " What are you doing?"

I said, "Knitting, Miss Barrett."

Betty Lloyd-Jones sitting on the revolving shelter at Bellair holding either Muckle Flugga or Scrabster. 1918.

"KNITTING!," she said. "Don't you know that's the GERMAN WAY TO KNIT? I absolutely forbid you to knit that way. **Real** knitting is Slip, Over, Under, Off."

" Yes, Miss Barrett," and I took the wool in the Other Hand and continued to knit in the idiom of my ancestors. Miss Barrett lasted about six weeks (the Kentish climate was too much for her), but Hélene stayed on for years, taught us French, and I contacted her some years later in Lausanne. To this day, I continue to knit with the wool over the left forefinger, but hold a strand of wool in either hand for all

50

colour-pattern knitting.

Miss Barrett was eventually succeeded by Elsie Goldney-Cary, who was deaf, but pretended not to be. They both taught by the method of Charlotte Mason, who had some kind of a school and governess-training institution at Ambleside in the Lake District. Miss Mason recommended our books, suggested courses of study, and damn her, insisted on the *theory of relating*, which means that you weren't taught facts, but read to, and were then expected to relate back what you had heard. A fine theory if the read stuff had been interesting. You also had to write in script, and paint without drawing first. This last simply resulted in my drawing in the outline of the flower, or what have you, with a brush and then filling in with colour as usual. Never mind; a very instructive technique, and errors were unallowable as they could not be erased.

Poor governesses, what a life they led; neither servants, guests, nor family. Poorly paid, and getting old all the time, and of course by this time the demand for them was already dwindling. Around the turn of the century, they were still quite common. All the money allotted for schooling was to be spent on the boys, who had to have been to a good and expensive school. What was left over was just enough to hire a governess who could be used for all the girls, as well as for the little boys. To have sent the children, even the girls, to the village school was completely unthinkable; they would have picked up a common accent. If you were lucky enough to live near a good boarding-school, you sent the children there as day-pupils, but "day-bugs" were despised by the boarders, and of course they were not of the same hardy breed, having comfortable homes to return to at night. So for us it was governesses for two years, and they taught us to write and figure neatly, and keep a nice tidy exercise book, and mind our P's and Q's.

CHAPTER FOUR

THE KNITTED MOEBIUS

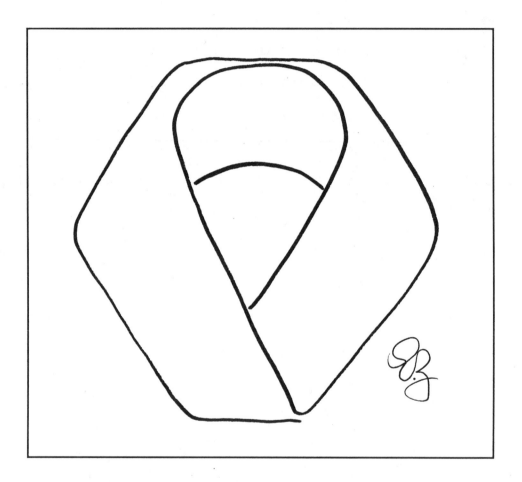

    The whole Moebius principle formed a large gap in my education until one day, at a knitting workshop, a student demonstrated it to us with a long skinny piece of paper, given one twist, and stuck together to form the MOEBIUS RING: a ring with *one* surface and *one* edge. She's nuts, you say; but make one for yourself, and see.

My knitting subconscious set to work right away, and lo, the Knitted Moebius was born in 1981. This is the first knitted garment, to our knowledge, ever to incorporate the Moebius principle. We used garter-stitch because of its wonderful attributes: both its sides are the same, it will not curl at the edges, and it can be woven seamlessly.

*From L to R: Lloie wearing a Mistake-Stitch * Moebius, knitted in 2-ply Icelandic Wool; Elizabeth in a Lace-Patterned Moebius in 1-ply Icelandic; and Meg in a 1-ply Icelandic garter-stitch version.
MISTAKE STITCH: K2, P2 on a multiple of 4 plus 1.

The first Moebius off the needles was, of course, a warm winter scarf, about 60" long, and it soon demonstrated its manifold characteristics: once around the neck with hands cuddled into the bottom fold, as into a muff; twice around the neck for very cold days; once around the neck, then letting the twist twist itself, and up over the head for an elegant hood (shown above); and finally, twice around the head for a super turban.

Couldn't it be made into one side of a sweater, we asked ourselves? But that lumpy bit at the side - how could it be coped with? I forget who came up with the answer...Cully, we think...Don't Bother To Join The Ends. Just make two halves with the turns at the shoulders, and join it at the sides and center back.

We immediately started to knit, and it worked! Of course not right away. A certain amount of shaping was necessary to make the lower edge hang properly, but that problem was soon solved. An unexpected bonus then appeared: it didn't matter which way out the thing was worn. Reversing it changed its form completely. Sew buttons or clasps on both inside and outside.

Who was this Moebius guy? The following was kindly contributed to our 1983 Wool Gathering by the engineer in the family, Meg's father-in-law, T. L. Swansen:

Many of us thought, when we finished geometry in high school, that we had a sufficient knowledge of the subject. There was some justification for this, since we were only exposed to the geometry of Euclid, with its points, lines, and planes. However, there is much more to geometry. The term Topology has been assigned to a most important branch of advanced geometry. Topology concerns itself with vast spaces in contrast to specific sizes and shapes of the Euclidean configurations, and uses more than the three dimensions of Euclid. To study these multi-dimensional spaces they have to be classified, and this requires an object to compare them to. This object has to have the unique property of having only ONE SURFACE, and this need was filled by the invention of the great Mathematician/Topologist, August Ferdinand Moebius (1790-1868).

The study of topology has continued its advance, and just this past year the famous four-dimensional conjecture of Jules Henri Poincaré has been proved. This last study produced a startling result in that there are other four-dimensional universes than our own. To date, it is not known if we will be able to "talk" with these other universes. However, in view of a possible meeting, Wool Gathering *feels it prudent to incorporate the Moebius Strip in a new sweater design because if such an encounter takes place, one should be properly dressed for the occasion.*

The questions arises as to how "Moebius" is pronounced. Since he was Swiss-German, he surely pronounced himself Meuh-Byoos, with the meuh as in the mooing of a cow. Some simplify matters by saying Mow-Byus. Some pronounce the Umlaut in American, saying Maybe-Us. We rather prefer the third method. After all, who should present this marvellous theory to the knitting public for the first time? Maybe us?

Let us begin with
THE ENDLESS SEAMLESS ONE-SURFACED, ONE-EDGED SHAWL-CAP-MUFF:

MATERIALS: About 9 oz of thick, or 4 oz of thin wool. A circular needle (or pair of needles) of a size to give you whatever **GAUGE** pleases you. That seems vague, but this is one instance where *fit* is not critical, and you are encouraged to work with the gauge that best suits the wool and texture you choose.

54

We use Icelandic wool for most of our scarves, as it is truly the world's warmest wool, and has the advantage of allowing you to work in 1-ply (for lace), 2-ply for medium-weight, or 3-ply for bulky.

OK.

CAST ON about 10" worth of stitches, plus 4 if you are working Built-In-I-Cord. Gifted knitters may want to use **Invisible Cast On** to facilitate the weaving at the end. Otherwise, be prepared to unpick your casting on.

Garter-stitch Moebius Scarf with Applied I-Cord added afterward. 1-ply Icelandic wool.

Begin knitting, remembering to choose a texture pattern that is reversible, as both sides of the finished scarf will show at once. We recommend garter-stitch for your first effort.

BUILT-IN-I-CORD BORDERS: *Knit to the last 3 stitches, wool forward, slip 3 purlwise, turn. Repeat from *.

At about 60", take out the casting on to reveal a row of stitches. Give one end of the piece HALF a turn, pin A to A, and B to B, and weave the ends together.

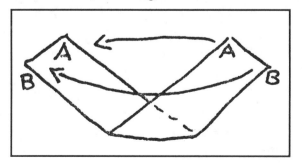

CONTRASTING I-CORD BORDER: On garter-stitch version, simply work all knit, slipping every first stitch. When piece is finished and woven, take a smaller d.p. needle and pick up one stitch for each ridge along the selvedge - about 12-15 stitches at a time. On regular-size needle, **CAST ON 3 stitches;** transfer them to the left needle; *K2 of them, slip 1, K1 of the picked-up stitches, psso. Replace the 3 stitches onto lefthand needle, and repeat from *. This makes a spectacular selvedge, and you arrive back where you started. Yes. Just ONE EDGE. Weave end of I-Cord to beginning - which cannot be done perfectly, as you are joining opposing pieces of stocking-stitch. Two of the stitches can be woven perfectly; fudge the third, and work a kind of duplicate stitch to give the appearance of perfection. Try the thing on, every which way. Are you bedazzled by your skill?

55

Before you begin your Moebius Jacket, consider some of your options:

What texture do you want to work in? Be sure it is something reversible.

Do you want the whole thing to be surrounded by **Built-In-I-Cord**?

Or do you want to work **Applied I-Cord** in a contrasting color after the jacket is finished?

Think about buttonholes: **Hidden I-Cord? Loop I-Cord? I-Cord Tab?** Perhaps no buttonholes, but a pewter clasp or two instead.

A useful swatch: a potholder surrounded by Built-In-I-Cord. See the two Short Rows in the middle?

If you should choose the Built-In- I-Cord version, I recommend that you knit up the swatch shown here.

SWATCH:

Begin with **I-CORD "CASTING ON"**: CAST ON 3 stitches. *K3, replace stitches onto left hand needle, and repeat from *. Yes, the wool will always be coming fom the last stitch on the needle, to be pulled across the back of the three stitches. This forms the tiny tube known as **I-Cord** (originally called Idiot Cord). Knit 12 rowlets of I-Cord. Leaving the 3 stitches on the needle, work back along the cord, knitting up one stitch for each row of cord. Take out the original casting on, and put those 3 stitches on the needle too. You have 12 knitted-up stitches in between a 3-stitch I-Cord on each end. Now work back and forth in garter-stitch as follows:

*K to within 3 stitches of end. Wool forward, slip last 3 purlwise, turn. Repeat from *
SHORT ROWS: K to the middle of the swatch, Wrap, Turn, work back. This is the same method used on stocking-stitch, BUT, when you knit back across and meet the wrap, ignore it. It is impossible to make short rows in garter-stitch invisible (one ridge suddenly becomes two), but it is least noticeable if you leave the wrap strangling the stitch; it resembles a purl bump. At 12 ridges, cast off as follows:
I-CORD CASTING OFF: *K2 cord stitches, slip the 3rd, K a stitch to be cast off, psso, replace the 3 stitches onto lefthand needle. Repeat from * across.
LOOP I-CORD BUTTONHOLE: After last cast off stitch, work plain I-Cord for 10-11 rows (rounds, actually). Weave to the 3 cord stitches on the potholder. You may leave the loop as it is, but in a buttonhole, the area at the base of the loop may stretch - so give it a twist, and secure it by sewing, or wrapping wool around it.

Stoo, modelling a Moebius Vest knitted in super thick Sheepsdown.

The Moebius Strip has been referred to as "The Riddle of the Universe", and we like the idea that a beginning knitter can easily produce this mystery for a first-time project (with, perhaps, some help in the weaving department).

One more thing. Many knitters, when hearing about the twist and join, have leaped to their feet to exclaim that they have produced inadvertant Moebius strips when joining their circular knitting. We had thought the same thing - and for a moment relished the idea of writing knitting instructions that would read: "Join Being Careful To Twist". Alas, that produces a 360 degree twist, and the Moebius requires a 180 degree twist.

Now for a jacket. This is not a true Moebius, as its ends are not joined, but the twist does bemusing things to the "collar".

THE MOEBIUS JACKET:
One of the greatest charms of this project is its extreme simplicity. No purling. No measurements except chest circumference. Two side seams. One back seam, and all that lovely I-Cord at the edges, which is so fascinating to work.
We have knitted 4 versions to date:
The 42" model in Sheepsdown shown at the left took eight 4oz skeins, @ 2.5 stitches to 1".
A 40" vest took five 4oz skeins of 2-ply Sheepswool, *or* Homespun *or* Fisherman Wool @ 5 stitches to 1".

57

A 34" jacket @ 4 stitches to 1" took exactly 4 skeins of Highland Wool.

A 2-ply Icelandic model; 39" around, @ a gauge of 4 stitches to 1", required five 3.5oz wheels of Icelandic.

SO:

Measure your favorite jacket around; multiply the inches times the GAUGE obtained with the wool and needles you plan to use; divide the result by 4.

Add 4 extra stitches if you plan to work Built-In-I-Cord-Borders.

CAST ON for half the back (in I-Cord?)

ALL ROWS (for Built-In-I-Cord): *K to the last 3 stitches, wool forward, slip 3 purlwise, turn. Repeat from *.

ALL ROWS (for Applied I-Cord added afterward): *Slip 1, K to end, turn. Repeat from *.

When piece is wanted length from lower edge to a few inches past the top of the shoulder, shape to prevent the Dreaded Frontal Droop:

*K to center of the piece, Wrap, turn, K back. Work 3 Ridges (6 rows) plain and repeat from * to within a few inches of lower front edge.

When front is about 2" longer than back (on the extra row side), **CAST OFF** in I-Cord along lower edge as follows: *K2, Slip 1, K1, psso. Repeat from * across to other corner, and weave I-Cord to I-Cord. Jacket is half done.

Make an identical piece. Study the drawings on this page, and keep your wits about you. Join at center back. Sew side seams, leaving a few inches open at lower edges if you like.

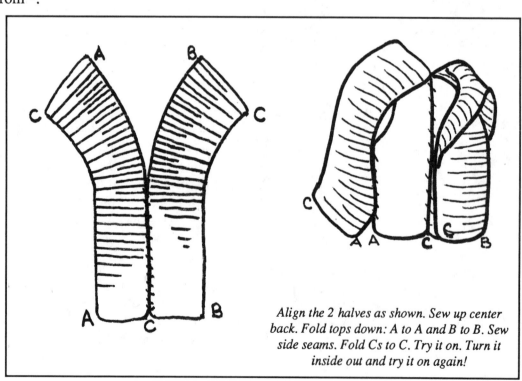

Align the 2 halves as shown. Sew up center back. Fold tops down: A to A and B to B. Sew side seams. Fold Cs to C. Try it on. Turn it inside out and try it on again!

OPTION: Our latest version eliminates the center back seam by casting on across the lower back edge from side to side. Knit to the shoulder height, then divide into R and L sides, and shape down the fronts. See to it that the <u>inside</u> edges get the Short Rows because when they are turned prior to sewing the side seams, they will become the <u>outside</u> edges.

APPLIED I-CORD BORDER:

With a contrasting color, work the same as the border on the scarf. But...

TO TURN CORNERS IN I-CORD:

Work to corner stitch; K all 3 I-Cord stitches without attaching. Attach corner stitch. Work a second unattached row; continue. This provides sufficient fabric to turn a good, sharp 90-degree corner.

I-CORD BUTTONHOLES, HIDDEN:

Work applied I-Cord to where you want a buttonhole. Work 3 rows of I-Cord without attaching, and slip 3 picked-up stitches off the left needle. Continue applying to next buttonhole site.

LOOP I-CORD BUTTONHOLES:

See swatch/potholder instructions on p 56.

When worn this way out, the lower edge of the "shawl collar" follows over the shoulder and becomes the side seam!

Turn it inside out, and the collar edge becomes the center back!

FREE-FORM I-CORD:

Meg came up with this a number of years ago, and there are several methods:

§ Work a length of free-standing I-Cord, and sew it on to form whatever design you like.

§ When applying I-Cord (as shown in this photo), work a length of plain I-Cord *unattached*, then continue applying. Form the long loop into a design, and tack it down.

§ With small d.p. needle, pick up stitches from the finished garment in either a wandering - or a carefully planned - path.

Applied Free-Form I-Cord at the center (seamless) back of a Moebius jacket.

Work applied I-Cord to the picked up stitches, and continue. You can roam all over the finished fabric, creating any imaginable design or shape.

New I-Cord applications keep popping up:

The I-Cord on the jacket in the above photo was worked on two stitches instead of three.

The next time you knit a free-standing I-Cord, try working K1, P1, K1 instead of all knit. You will see three stitches form a four-sided square length of cord!

Kathy Lynch "unvented" **Intarsia I-Cord For Circular Knitting**: Cast on in one color for a hat. For vertical stripes of contrasting-color I-Cord spaced around the cap, attach bobbins at each wanted location, and knit one stitch in the contrasting (bobbin) color. Next round, M1, knit bobbin stitch, M1 at each location. On ensuing rounds you will work the 3 bobbin stitches in I-Cord. See? It is perfectly adapted for this...on each new round, the wool is left hanging at the Wrong End of the I-Cord - which, in reality, is the Right end! Wonderful.

OPPOSITE PAGE: Elizabeth's pencil sketch of Lloie and Meg climbing trees at Butternut Lake, Wisconsin. August 1952

61

Elizabeth
Age 16

. . . Digressions

Mummy was supposed to be starting married life on a comparative shoe-string, but until I was 12 there was Lizzie and Nanny, Mrs. Sackett for the heavy cleaning, the Laundry came for the dirty clothes, and on occasion a Mrs. Whoosis to do the sewing. I will say that Mummy always had a huge piled up mending basket, and she looked after us on the maids' day off (which left her prostrated), read to us, listened to our prayers, and sometimes took us for walks. Otherwise I'm not sure what she did do. It's hard for me to believe now, that in those days the really tough moment of the day for the Lady of the House was right after breakfast, when the cook came in for orders, and the meals of the day had to be decided. Then she attended to her correspondence, as telephones were a rare and slightly extravagant thing (one lifted up the receiver and shouted "Are you there?). So, many little notes whizzed back and forth between friends and acquaintances, carried usually by the governess and children on their walks. Next, I sup-pose, she did the flowers, until a bell rang for luncheon. When the eating part of luncheon was over she simply got up and walked out of the room, and the dirty dishes were never seen again. A nap then, I imagine, and perhaps a tea-party, and dinner appeared magically at about 7 or 8 o'clock. Poor Mummy. All this was to stop for her. Instead of servants becoming more plentiful and leisure even more elaborate, servants dwindled to Mrs. Sackett, and then to nothing, and she was doing her own washing in a non-electric machine.

Mummy

Anyway, it was 1919, and Pop was going to work in a bank in the city every day. Poor Pop, he never really had a career, but puttered and frittered along like a great many "ex-officers" of that day. Fortunately he and Mummy had a little money between them, some of it tied up in trust; enough to keep us scratching along, but not enough to pay boarding-school bills for a trio of girls and to run a house with servants. There were several schemes brooded out for Pop, but they all seemed to run into difficulties, with Somebody Getting The Better of Him, and Pop trying again at something else. He had the talent, and more important, the temperament for an actor, but Grandpa Greenwood frowned on it, and let's face it, Mummy would not have made an actor's wife. However she did have the insight to see that this would have been a solution, although she never got so far as actually promoting it. Instead she got carried away with the idea of "The Community Kitchen", or as it was later called "Meals By Motor".

"Grandpa" Benjamin Isaac Greenwood driving at Shoreham, Kent 1908.

Actually, looking back, I realize that M by M was quite an outstanding achievement (now suceeded by the London "Meals On Wheels"). It consisted of a large kitchen, ablaze with chef, cooks, and kitchen-maids, as well as a modest fleet of motor-vans, which delivered whole meals in heated aluminum containers to families who had neither the skill nor the will to cook their own meals. At the time, however, M by M had been one of my chief menaces at Oaklea (my boarding school, about which more in a moment), since to have a parent behind any commercial counter was *infra dig* of the gravest blood, and had caused the other girls to sneer at me. Mummy had dreamed it all up herself, with, I imagine, lukewarm support from my Pop, just returned from the Royal British Navy. She was strongly backed by her family (Uncles Benny and Paul and Aunts Pete and Carol). Gramps (Benjamin Isaac Greenwood) approved of the undertaking, I think, and probably invested in it. He was a very prosperous old boy, living at Coombe Hollow, near Shoreham in Kent, and married to his second wife Alice Passmore ("Auntie Alice").

Coombe Hollow was a spectacular place; 7 bedrooms (at least), an indoor fountain in the hall, and downstairs breakfast room, dining-room, study, lounge, drawing-room and glass-room-full-of-flowers, not to mention twenty acres of strongly sloping meadows with two cows, and endless glass-houses. The chief gardener was named Swasiland, and I used to play with his kids.

When my dear "Auntie Granny Grace" (my mother's mother) died, she was succeeded by Auntie Alice, which displeased the whole family except perhaps Gramps. (For instance, it was she who suggested that I cease my new passion for crochet and return to knitting, since crochet was just "done by the servants"!)

Auntie Granny Grace was "talented", and I was supposed to have received my drawing ability from her. I can still see her dabbing away at a field of poppies, giving me a brush loaded with Scarlet Lake, letting me put in three large ones, and signing a wavery "B" to it for me. I was three, and treasured that water color for years.

By 1923, when I was thirteen or so, the Community Kitchen became transmogrified into Meals by Motor, and had opened a branch in Margate, four miles to the east of us, which was run by Nellie Carpenter, a girlhood friend of Mummy's. The next branch was in London, on the Finchley Road at Swiss Cottage, and Mummy always said that it would have been successful if Margate hadn't been dragging it down. By this time, I had been sent to boarding-school at Buckhurst Hill in Epping Forest.

Auntie Granny Grace Greenwood

The Drawing-Room at Coombe Hollow

The school was called Oaklea, and though it wasn't at all a bad one, and I learned quite a bit there of this and that, it has frequently featured in my worst dreams. I was a dreary child and nobody liked me much, which upset me. There were about 40 boarders and 100 "daybugs", and when the girls formed crocodile, to go to church or on a walk, I was always the one left to walk with the mistress, or with the other two girls whom nobody liked. When sides were picked in games, I was always chosen very near the last, and I was absolutely no good at games either. The school was very cold, and fresh air was encouraged. Bedroom windows were always open it seemed, and we weren't allowed to wear our blazers in the evenings unless the thermometer read below 60° Fahrenheit.

We learned as little as in any other school, but at least we learned grammar and spelling from much reading, and from being among people who spoke properly. Our handwriting developed nicely; we were always working on it, and copying new ways of making cute letters from each other. I spent a great deal of time drawing and filling in the drawings with water-colours, and I was reasonably good. My other talent was playing the piano, at which I was about third or fourth best, until we were all eclipsed and far outstripped by the advent of Wendy Tyler, who had a "natural inborn talent". Knitting was not a part of the school curriculum, but if you wanted to knit, no one would stop you. I remember knitting a white and yellow horizontally striped sweater, and was encouraged in this by Miss Ben, the housekeeper. I also read a lot and turned out corny little poems. So, all in all, I was branded as "artistic", and though unpopular, was nevertheless as conceited as ever.

It was a quite fairly miserable time, and all I really wanted to do was stay in Birchington and go to the public central school in Margate. The girls at Oaklea were, I suppose, nearly all children of professional middle-class families, and I felt it necessary to go to enormous pains to hide the fact that my parents were in trade. I could not have friends to stay with me, and when my parents came to school I was of course ashamed of them, as I suppose most of us were, in one way or another. However, my stinky, perverse old Pop really went out of his

Elizabeth's pencil drawing of Artist at Work.
Munich. 1932.

way to be difficult, and would only
appear in a disgracefully dirty old
Burberry and a shabby cloth cap,
making off-beat remarks, and showing
us up in front of the mistresses.

My own clothes were far from
unobtrusive. In the interests of econ-
omy, Mummy did not buy the regular
uniform at Daniel Neal's, such as all
the other kids wore, but would, with
enormous labour, try to copy the
uniform in what she held to be better
quality material. Then in regard to the
clothes out of uniform, into which we
were allowed to change in the evenings, I was let to "have my head"
entirely in their choice. I had the most
motley collection of garments - I
particularly remember a knitted silk
dress handed down from Auntie Pete -
and must have looked a regular little
scarecrow. At least I made one good
lifelong friend, Marjorie Smardon, but
she left when I had been there only a
year. My next and other friend was
Moire (pronounced Moya) Atkinson,
and, through having recently become
aware (in 1986) of the existence of the
Oaklea Old Girls League, I found Moire
again, and we have corresponded and

Elizabeth, age fourteen.

seen each other since. Perhaps Oaklea's most famous graduate of my period is
Rachel Kempson, who entered at the same time I did and has since become Mrs.
Michael Redgrave, mother of Vanessa and Lynn, and a recognised actress in her
own right. She was one of the few who was friendly towards me during my Oaklea
period.

Moire Atkinson also had rather to hide the fact that she lived in a row-
house, as her father was town-clerk of Walthamstow. This was a good job, and he
was an able man, but he had to live in his district, which was a rather slummy one,
and anyway Moire and I considered that the word "clerk" had rather low connota-
tions. My mind boggles now at how skilled in class consciousness we and all our
schoolmates were. But there you have it. School itself was not too difficult: a native
French teacher, and the art teacher really quite nice. Until, that is, I found her
poking in my desk, having heard rumour that it concealed *male letters!* From that
day on I treated her very coldly. Rather annoying for her I think, and hoped, since I
was one of the better draftsmen of my age.

After Marge left, school became duller and duller, so my parents kindly allowed me to escape at about fifteen. I immediately went to stay with my dear FLAG aunts (as we called Pop's sisters **F**lorence, **L**loie, **A**pay, and **G**ertrude), and spent as much time with them as I possibly could since my parents were totally involved with "Meals By Motor" in Hampstead.

My mother, in her youth, had been to a Swiss pensionnat (small boarding school), and it was now decided that I follow in her footsteps. So off I went to Lausanne on Lake Geneva, all by myself.

I knew next to no French, despite my governess and Oaklea, and, becoming hungry at the train-change in Paris, I scraped together the sentence of "Jer ver monjay", of which I was quite proud! Arriving at Lausanne in Switzerland, I discovered that there was no one to

Elizabeth, her Father Herbert Lloyd-Jones , Romper, and Rattler in the family motor car. c 1924

meet me, but I had the wit to say to a taxi driver, "Jer ver allay a Clare von Tane", Clairfontaine being the name of the remains of the pensionnat attended by my mother at approximately my age.

He drove me near the lake, to a large building guarded by a huge fence with a frightening ten-foot iron gate. He rang the bell for me, and out came a young housemaid, armed with cab-money and an enormous key to unlock the gate. She dragged my luggage into the house and led me to Mlle Pelichet, the head (and only) mistress. It turned out she had an arrangement with my mother that she would take me for free if my mother would whip up some English students for her. This arrangement did not work very well, so that I was for some time the only student, until a mixed bag of German, Czechoslovakian, and some English students trickled in.

In the morning I, and the other few Pelichet students, suffered French classes guided by a Reverend Monsieur Pelichet (brother of Mlle). Luckily for me, since the main reason for going to Lausanne was to attend the local art school, I was permitted to escape the pensionnat each afternoon.

It was a great treat to stand upright before a real easel with a genuine palette over my left arm. The Art School (run by Monsieur Rambert) was quite a good one, and I learned a lot, having, up until then, held my pencil and paintbrush like a pen.

Several of the students told me that it wasn't a very *good* art school, and that there was a vastly superior one in München in South Germany. So when my year was over and I returned home for the summer, I started pestering my parents to send me there, which they docilely did. They bought me a ticket and popped me into the train for Dover. From thence across the Channel to France, and into a train for Germany, where I shared my 24-hour (no-kidding) trip to Munich with an utterly charming American.

Arriving in Munich, I was met by the sister of my former Swiss governess.

"Und vere are you going to stay ?" she asked.

Art School in Lausanne, Switzerland. Betty, with crossed legs, and M. Rambert behind her. c. 1927.

I showed her a page cut by Mummy from a German magazine listing all manner of addresses in Munich. She was quite shocked, as many of them were rather obviously houses of doubtful activity!

She offered to take me to a very nice place she knew of in Northern Munich where they not only served a good lunch, but also took in lodgers.

So we hopped into a trolley, and hopped out again in Schwabing. It was indeed a nice place but too expensive for my budget. However, the kind owner said that I might stay there temporarily until I found an apartment. She showed me to a bedroom, where I tottered into bed for 24 hours solid sleep.

The next day she asked me why had I come to Munich?

"I'm going to the Art Academy," I said.

"Well," she said, "A young man is coming to lunch who hopes to be accepted by a *preparatory*-school for the Academy; I think he can help you."

He certainly could. Nobody was accepted by the *"Akademie"* without thorough technical training, and he took me to the Heymannschule, where we were both admitted. Heymann himself was an absolute treasure, and charged me a preposterously low fee, to my delight. My introducer then said that he was moving out of his furnished room and imagined that they would take me in his place. They would. DM 30 a month!

Elizabeth's Pencil sketch of a Bavarian mountain farmyard. c. 1930.

CHAPTER FIVE

THE KNITTED BOG JACKET

The Bog Shirt floats to the surface of a positive quagmire of fact, legend, superstition and doubt. The best known artifact was retrieved from the preservative depths of a Danish bog; the tannic acid in peat bogs will preserve anything, including the wearer of the Bog Shirt himself. There are assorted grisly details, as well as fascinating deductions and conclusions derived from common factors connecting the deaths of numerous people who have been discovered in bogs. To pursue this, ask your library to track down a copy of a book called *The Bog People*.

71

We, however, concern ourselves with the leather garment worn by one of the victims. It is said that a hide is godgiven material for a Bog Shirt, being more or less rectangular. But surely this super simple shape must go back to dimmer ages. Strange only is the fact that, as far as we know, none had ever been KNITTED. We intend to take care of that.

Weavers have known about the magical Bog Shirt for years. Its shape allows them to make a sleeved jacket from a square piece of woven goods without cutting away a single precious inch of fabric.

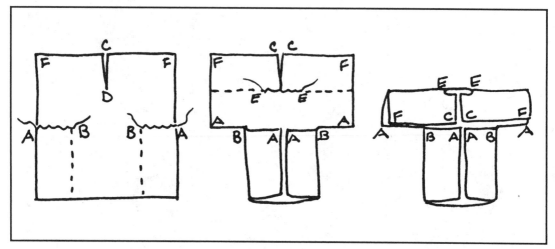

The Bog Shirt.

Try this with a square piece of paper:
>At the halfway point on either side, cut in for 1/4 of the width, A-B.
>At center top, cut in for 1/4 of the depth, C-D.
>Fold As at Bs so that they meet at the center.
>Fold Cs down to A-Bs, making a small sideways snip at E-E for the neck.
>Make two seams at A-B-A, and there is your Bog Shirt.

Weavers must cut into their fabric at E for the neck, and at A-B for the underarms. They will also have a visible seam where C-F meets A-B.

Knitters have the ability to produce a *Seamless Bog*, with an assortment of tailoring embellishments. First, here is the Basic Bog:

THE KNITTTED BOG JACKET

EXPOSITION: Get a 24" circular needle, or a pair of long needles, and cast on sufficient stitches for the body circumference at the lower edge. This number of stitches, Circumference Times Gauge, will be your KEY NUMBER [K], and all future shaping will be percentages of [K].

You may use garter-stitch, or any non-curling fabric that you like, keeping in mind that there is quite a bit of weaving in store. I strongly recommend garter-stitch for this garment, as it is such a logical choice. Not only is it non-curling, reversible, and easy to weave perfectly, but it also permits the simplest of mathematical computations: 2 rows equal 1 ridge; 10 stitches and 10 ridges equals a perfect square, as will 178 stitches and 178 ridges. As you can see in the drawing, we are working with halves and quarters in both directions: vertical ridges and horizontal stitches. See how well suited garter-stitch is to the mathematical computations required to produce a custom-fitted jacket?

Knit away, slipping all first stitches, until the piece is half as long as it is wide: 50% of [K]...or longer for ectomorphs.

OPTION: You are now at the underarm and it is time to incorporate Phoney Seams at the sides, if you wish, from B to lower edge. These are particularly pleasing in garter-stitch, forming one vertical row of stocking stitch, and giving a nice, tailored appearance. Also, you have the option of making the phoney seams themselves reversible! (see ahead)

A partial Bog Jacket. The left half is finished and woven; the right half is waiting for the "Thumb Trick" wool to be removed so as to weave the body and sleeve. Note the inside of the Phoney Seam on the right.

NOW: With a length of contrasting wool, *knit the last 1/4 of the stitches on the row (25% of [K]), replace them on the lefthand needle, and re-knit them in the main color. Repeat from * at the other end. (You may know this as "The Thumb Trick" used in mittens.) This maneuver forms part of the horizontal joining of sleeves and fronts later on.

Continue straight for another 25% of [K], and you are 3/4 finished. For sneaky shoulder shaping, see Embellishments on next page.

The left side has been woven; the right side has just had the contrasting wool removed at the midpoint; raw stitches still on the needle ready to be woven

At center, knit 15% of [K] stitches with contrasting color for the neck E-E. Replace the stitches on lefthand needle, re-knit in main color, and (√) continue on half the stitches for one side of the front.

When the **total length** of the piece is equal to the width, or [K] (meaning that you have as many garter-stitch ridges as there were cast-on stitches), repeat from (√) for other half of front.

Take out the spare pieces of wool at the midpoint, fold the sides to the center, fold the top down, and weave F-C to A-B-A.

Loosely cast off the neck stitches.

That's it for the Bald and Uninteresting version, but hang on, here comes :

BOG SHIRT EMBELLISHMENTS THAT ONLY KNITTERS CAN DO:

LONGER SLEEVES

The sleeve, left to itself, falls rather inelegantly at the elbow. On one version, I simply picked up the stitches around the lower sleeve edge and worked additional garter-stitch to a 3/4 sleeve-length.

But this idea came from Meg: when you have worked the "Thumb Trick" insertion at the underarms, in Main Color, Cast On Invisibly - at either end - as many extra stitches as you feel you will need... perhaps 12-13% of [K]... to form the longer sleeves. You will then be working from X to X. You may want to narrow the cuffs as you go, by

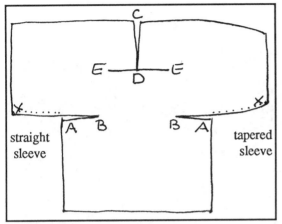

working short rows every few ridges as follows: *work to within 4-5" of edge, wrap, turn, and repeat from *. Work the wraps every 2-4 ridges.

For gradual shaping, stagger the distance of the wraps from the selvedge.

For an obvious narrow cuff, keep the wraps in the same place each time.

SHOULDER SHAPING:

Since the Bog Shirt is a folk-garment with typical kimono shoulders, you may want to shape these a bit. Start after about 1/3 of the sleeve rows (A-F) have been knitted. Mark 25% of [K] at the center. This seems a bit narrow, but we are allowing for stretch in the shoulder width. On the other hand, if you plan to add shoulder pads, you will want to establish the shoulder "seams" farther apart.

Identify the *first* and *last* of these marked stitches with safety pins, and slip them purlwise on the wrong side. This forms a vertical line of stocking stitch on the right side, and will denote the "armhole" line. *(see photo on next page)*

Liesl wearing a Long-Sleeved Bog.

On the right side, every second row, M(ake) 1, *outside* the marked stitches. Repeat this 5% of [K] times, then work straight to shoulder top, continuing to slip the marked stitches on the wrong side.

After the neck, the shoulder shaping is worked in reverse by *decreasing* next to the shoulder line every other row. This all causes the sleeve cap to shape itself pleasantly, but without exaggeration.

COLLAR:

Remove the spare wool from E-E. Pick up all stitches and work back and forth, decreasing one stitch at the beginning of each row for 5-7 ridges - or wanted height for collar.

If you plan to add Applied I-Cord for the final trim, leave the raw collar stitches on a needle or a piece of wool.

75

Close-up of shoulder shaping and collar. The I-Cord was applied afterward, and there are two hidden buttonholes on the left.

I-CORD BORDERS:

Starting at one side "seam", on the wrong side, with smaller double-pointed needle, in a contrasting color: PICK UP one stitch for each cast-on stitch along lower edge (about 12-15 stitches at a time).

On regular-size needle, CAST ON 3 stitches in the border color. Transfer the 3 stitches to the d.p. needle, and *K2, slip 1, K1, psso. Replace the 3 stitches onto the small needle, and repeat from *.

When you get to the lower front **corner**, turn it as follows: Work all three I-Cord stitches without attaching them; attach corner stitch; work all three I-Cord stitches without attaching again. Continue on.

By inserting the 2 extra rows of Cord, you have provided sufficient fabric to turn a nice sharp 90° corner.

Now, as you work your way up the front, you will be picking up one stitch for each <u>ridge</u> along the selvedge.

Work the I-Cord Buttonholes of your choice. (See preceding chapter for the **Loop I-Cord**, and the **Hidden I-Cord buttonholes**.)

SHORT ROWS:

To make the back slightly longer than the front, work 2-3 sets of well-spaced short rows across the back only. See preceding chapter for garter-stitch Short Rows.

AFTERTHOUGHT POCKETS:

It is often difficult to anticipate (while you are knitting), exactly where you will want the pockets to fall, so wait until the jacket is finished. Try it on and decide where the pockets will be most useful. Mark the center of the wanted opening with a safety-pin, and mark the mirror stitch on the other side.

SNIP the marked stitch, and unravel 8-10 stitches in either direction.

Pick up lower stitches, and CAST OFF in I-Cord. *(see last chapter).*

Pick up upper stitches and work back and forth in stocking stitch for an inch, keeping the 4 edge stitches in garter-stitch to prevent curling. Now begin to increase one stitch at the beginning of each row until pocket is nice and wide. Knit straight to wanted depth of pocket (working a few decreases to round bottom corners, if wanted). Cast Off and tack down. Darn in wool ends from cut opening.

This produces a pocket with a small, neat opening - but a useful, roomy interior.

Clockwise from top left: √ *A Long-sleeved Bog, 35" circumference. It took 1, 3.5oz wheel each of Cream and Blacksheep, and 6 wheels of grey 2-ply Icelandic.* √ *Homespun Bog. 5, 4oz skeins of Quoddy Blue and 1 skein Plum Homespun, plus one skein Navy Blue Fisherman. 36" around.* √ *42" Adult Bog took 9, 4oz skeins Highland Wool.* √ *The Baby Bog took 4oz Shetland wool, and is 26" around the lower edge, decreasing to 18" around chest.*

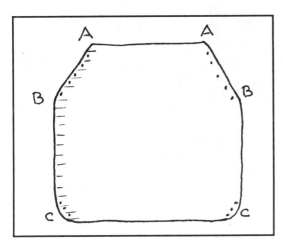

Afterthought Pocket

WAIST SHAPING:

This can be seen on the Long Sleeved and the Homespun Bogs in the photo above.

Several inches below wanted waistline, work to within 4 stitches of "seam" line. K2 tog, K5, SSK. Repeat at other side. (Stitch #3 of the K5 should be the Phoney Seam stitch.) Repeat twice more - allowing about 1/2" vertically between decreases. At 1/2" above the waistline, reverse the foregoing, and increase the stitches back up to [K], 4 at a time.

PHONEY SEAMS:

These are a great treat to work in garter-stitch, and provide a permanent fold at the sides. If you have shaped the sides of the jacket, this seam emphasizes and embellishes that shaping. Just before the insertion of the contrasting wool for the "Thumb Trick", find the exact side stitch, and drop it down to the casting on. Now, with a crochet hook, hook it up again, Two Stitches Together at a time, instead of the 2 and 1 for a stocking-stitch Phoney Seam.

REVERSIBLE PHONEY SEAMS:

These can be worked on garter-stitch as follows: Drop the seam stitch. Notice how the resulting ladders seem to separate themselves into front- and -back ladders? With a crochet hook, hook up every *front* ladder, one for one (in reality, this is every other one). Then turn the work over, pick up a thread from the fabric, pretend it is a stitch, and hook up all the **back** ladders, one for one. Isn't that nice?

You gain total reversibility, but lose the automatic fold that a single Phoney Seam causes; with a seam on both sides, it now doesn't know which way to fold.

The Baby Bog from the back.

THE BABY BOG

This cute babies' jacket is knitted in Shetland Wool at a gauge of 6 stitches to 1". The main feature is the gathered back *(see photo)* which permits the jacket to fit loosely and comfortably over the baby's bottom.

The [K] is 100, but, to produce the gathers, **CAST ON 160** (or 60% [K] too many).

At about 1" shy of underarm (approximately 7" from cast on edge), decrease away the 60 stitches across the back only, as follows: K20, K2 tog across back to within 20 sts of other end, K20.

The "armhole" delineation on this model is worked in Purl instead of Knit, and dimples in nicely, as you can see in the photo to the left. Work the last inch in a becoming color, and work the Applied I-Cord in the same color.

The Stylish Stripes on the prototype model occurred because I ran out of wool (it can happen to anyone). We liked the effect, and have added them to each subsequent version, proving the Great Truth that the words *DESIGN* and *MISTAKE* are often synonymous.

If the foregoing pages **bog**gle your brain, and you would feel more comfortable with abbreviated, stitch-by-stitch instructions, here you are:

BOG JACKET IN CHILD'S SIZES

GAUGE: 5 stitches to 1". Get it right. **MATERIALS:** 4 (5) 4oz skeins Homespun, Fisherman, 2-ply Sheepswool, or any wool that yields you this gauge. A 24" circular needle of a size to give you the above gauge (about #5-6). 1 smaller d.p. needle for I-Cord. **SIZES:** 24" (28") circumference at chest.

With 24" needle, **CAST ON** 120 (140) sts, or [K]. Work back and forth in garter-stitch, slipping all 1st sts, until piece is 60 (70) ridges, or 12" (14") long: 50% of [K].

K 90 (105) stitches. Now, with contrasting color wool, knit the remaining 30 (35) stitches. Replace the sts onto left needle, and re-knit in main color. Repeat at other end.

Continue straight until piece is 90 (105) ridges, or 18" (21") from beginning: 75% of [K].

At center, K18 (22) stitches in contrasting color for neck (E-E). Replace sts onto left needle. Continue on half the total sts: 60 (70) stitches.

When total length is 120 (140) ridges, or 24" (28") - in other words [K] - put stitches on thread and work other half.

Take out contrasting wools. Weave F-C to A-B-A. Cast off neck.

There's your Bog Jacket. Look over the list of embellishments on the last few pages and add some, or all, of them to your *next* Bog Jacket.

*A page of head studies from Elizabeth's sketch book
at the Heymannschule.*

80

The Art of Elizabeth Zimmermann

Fair Isle Yoke Sweater with Henley Neck

above
Knitted Dickeys

right
Apple Branch
July, 1985

watercolor
original size 6" x 8"

83

Farm, south of Granton, Wisconsin.
April, 1975.
watercolor original size 9" x 12"

below
Norwegian Mittens

The Moebius Group

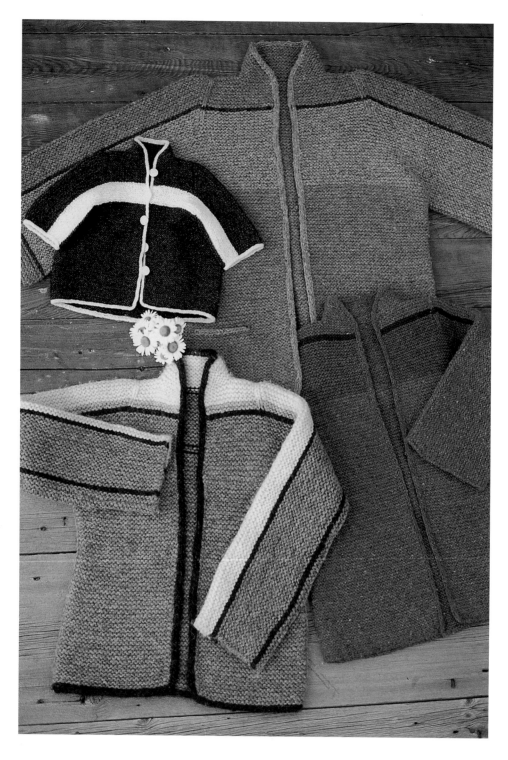

The Bog Group

right
Wild Flowers
Bernried, Germany.
c. 1932

watercolor
original size 4.5" x 6"

below
The Fraueninsel
Chiemsee, Bavaria.
Spring, 1932

watercolor
original size 6" x 5"

above
Moccasin Socks

left
Rose Hips

watercolor
original size 4" x 4"

88

Pie Are Square Shawls

above
Fair Isle Yoke

left
Arnica, 1935.

watercolor
original size 6" x8"

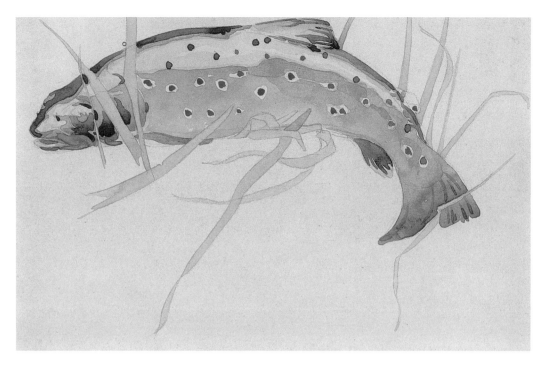

above

Brook Trout. Bernried, Germany. 1934.

watercolor   original size   7.5″ x 4.75″

below

The Three & One Group

91

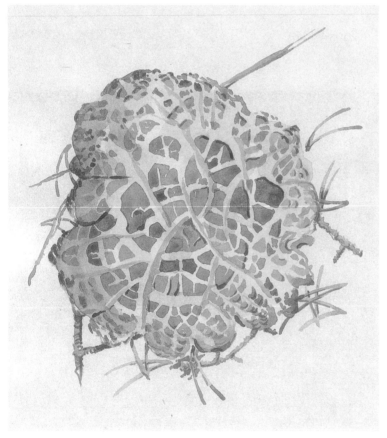

above
*Three & One
Cardigans*

left,
Garter Stitch Border

right,
Triple I-Cord Border

left
*Mushroom.
Lake Arethusa,
Canada. 1973.*

*watercolor
original size   6" x 7"*

92

right
Wild Geranium.
Canada. 1985

watercolor
original size 7" x 8"

below
Moebius Scarves

Norwegian Sweaters

above
Nakomis
Saskatchewan.
Canada. 1972

watercolor
original size 9" x 12"

right
Wild Flower
c. 1934

watercolor
original size 3" x 4"

95

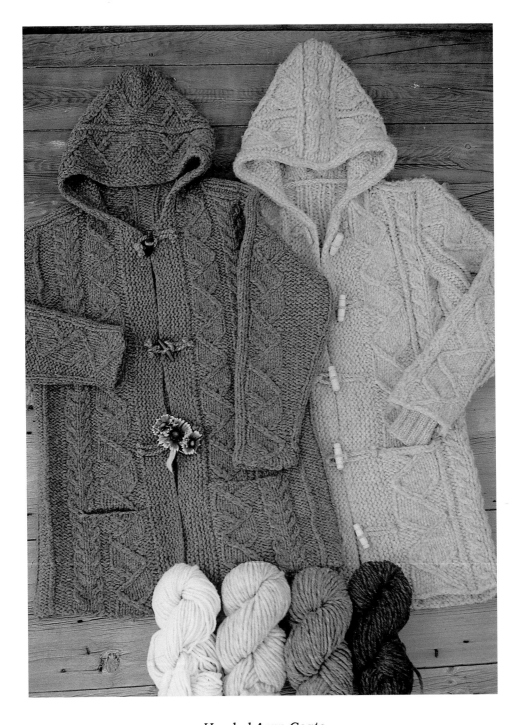

Hooded Aran Coats

96

Pencil drawing of a model at the Heymannschule
München. 1930

Water Lily. Bavaria, 1931

. . . Digressions

I now began a heavenly period at the Hey-mannschule, the pre-Akadamie Art School on the Turkenstrasse in Munich. There must have been well over 30 students on its high fifth floor, all drawing away in charcoal from live models. There was an art-supply store on the block, and soon I acquired proper paper, charcoal, and an effective eraser. Bliss had set in. The students were all of them talented and well-trained; many German and a few Americans. My chief friend was the fascinating and delightfully pleasant American Charlotte Jantzen. She discovered how little money I had each month, and we'd buy our lunches at a most economical bakery next door and consume them in the studio, all by ourselves. All the Heymann students were working with great conscientiousness but were, most of them, years away from an exam possibly to be accepted by the Academy.

The weekly town market in Munich.

It was a good year. Munich is a charming town, and I gradually started to absorb small bits of the German language. "Grüss Got" came first. This was Heymann's greeting every morning when he emerged from behind the thick curtains into the studio, preceded by his two terriers: "Guten *Morgen* meine damen; guten *Morgen* meine herren." I was daunted, to say the least, by the German language with its three genders and incredibly complicated words and accents. Bavarians roll their r's against their front teeth, not halfway down their throats as do so many Germans from farther North. Thus I gradually started to absorb, and give rather awkward tongue to, the Bavarian dialect, which has stayed with me to this day, often to the diversion of Germans from other parts of the country.

*Marge Smardon and Elizabeth
Art Students in Munich.*

Can you doubt that I returned to England after the first year thoroughly besotted by Munich and its inhabitants, let alone my acquired language and drawing-skill. I visited Marge Smardon (from my Oaklea days) who had also been at an art school in Reading. I set about persuading her that art school in Munich was unbeatable, and before long we set off for Bavaria together.

99

We found a nice reasonable bed-sitting-room at the top of an old building in Schwabing, and settled down to work and learn at Heymann's. Every morning in would come "The Terrace"; a cleaning-lady called Therese, saying "Yetzt komm I(ch)" to clean up our room, so that we didn't mind one bit climbing four sets of stairs to reach it. I soon evolved the idea of knitting away on sweaters and jerseys which I then exchanged at the woolshop for *more* wool and a little change to knit models which I could exchange at the woolshop for *more* wool. Ad infinitum. It was very rewarding to see my knitted pieces exhibited in the shop-window at pleasing prices.

Pretty soon Fasching was upon us to our surprise and delight. Fasching? The name for the 3-4-week annual Munich Carnival; parties and balls all over town, in evening dress or inspired self-made costumes. One day a dear but not particularly loved male acquaintance invited us to a Carnival-party. Marge didn't hesitate to refuse politely, with valid excuses; I, by some incredible instinct, however, accepted. And here I met Kurt Scharff, and we talked about this and that and skiing, which I loved, and had learned the rudiments of during my stay in Switzerland.

The very next day we met - with our skis - and set off by train to the Schliersee, which is surrounded by mountains. Up we walked to a nice building, and had a good lunch, which we enjoyed. Then came the next move; to ski down to the valley.

We lashed on our skis and set off downhill, me inelegantly determined to turn as many difficult corners as possible. On the very first turn, down I went, and couldn't get up again. Damn! A hurt ankle.

Kurt immediately called up the rescue-squad, who affixed me to a sled, and skillfully transported me down to the valley, Kurt skiing behind, carrying my skis. We took the train back to Munich and went straight to the nearest hospital, which diagnosed a cracked ankle and put me to bed, while Kurt set off to tell Marge what had happened.

The hospital took great and good care of me for about a week, during which I received visits and

Elizabeth in Fasching Costume. 1931

100

loving gifts from Marge and other friends. Among them was a spectacular bunch of flowers from a guy whom I'd met at the party where I met Kurt. The "guy" was rather a crum whom I did not fancy by any means. How-ever, upbringing came to the fore, and I wrote him a nice little thank you note (one of the most important moves of my life).

This "guy" worked in a bank, and had felt himself unable to resist boasting to a fellow worker about the genuine British thank you note. The fellow-worker was intrigued by the funny Limey handwrit-ing (in bright green ink, no less), and said that since he was able to borrow his father's little car, he could drive the note-receiver and flower-giver up to Sch-wabing where this wounded-ankle Limey lived with her friend Margery. Arrangements settled.

Arnold Ernst Zimmermann. 1931

After about ten days the hospital released me-and-my-ankle, and Marge took me up to Schwabing, where we somehow struggled up to our room in the big old appartment house. Now in those days people loved to dance, and Marge and I had a gramophone and some quite fashionable British records, to which we danced each weekend. In fact all kinds of nice people would drop in on a Saturday afternoon, and we would foxtrot like crazy. Well; this was where the guys from the bank turned up one Saturday while we were all dancing. The bell sounded, and I went to open the door. Who should I see but

Cast picture of student theatre group; Elizabeth at left in white dress, and Marge at right as maid, holding roses. München c. 1932

the guy to whom I'd written the flower-thank-you-note. Behind him, in overcoat and trilby hat was Another Guy, who imprinted himself on my conscious and subconscious from that moment on. Yes; that's who it was; Arnold Zimmermann.

I think I will say no more, except that here he and I are, in 1989, in our beloved Wisconsin Schoolhouse, parents and grandparents, passionate motorcyclist and passionate handknitter. All this may very well be, as my dear old father would have said, "A bald and uninteresting narrative", but Arnold and I have been happily married since 1937.

In any case, here was the end of my dear little single, lonely life, enlivened only by Marge and my Lloyd-Jones and Greenwood families.

*Arnold and Elizabeth and
Arnold's Scott Motorcycle. c 1932*

Arnold and Elizabeth

Well, I continued to work hard at my drawing from life at the Heymannschule to the point where I put my name down for the entrance-exam at the Art Akademie. Arnold, whose father and ancestors had been active and famous in Munich's art circles, introduced me to Professor Hess, who taught at the Akademie. He looked at my drawings, and commented favourably on them, saying he thought I would enjoy his class. So I took the exam, entered the Hessklasse, enjoying myself immensely, and continued at the Akademie for the next few years. Standards were high , and I learned a great deal.

*Arnold and Elizabeth and
Arnold's BMW motorcycle. c 1985*

One of the more spectacular events of my life took place in the summer of 1932. An English girl I knew at school told me she couldn't take a job she had been offered in Czechoslovakia, and that maybe I could. But first I would have to pass muster with a Countess Zeppelin, who lived in Munich. I must have passed, as before long I received a date and an address in Western Czechoslovakia. I was hired. I hurried back to England where I changed my wardrobe to all the good clothes I could find, including (mercifully) several evening dresses. Then I crossed the channel, France, and Germany, and left the train in Eger, just over the Western Czechoslovakian border. There an elegant lady awaited me, all dressed in black: the Countess Eltz. I joined her in an impressive horse-and-carriage, and off we trotted in an Easterly direction.

She was pleased that I spoke German, and assured me that Czechoslovakian would not be necessary. My chief duty would be to speak English as much as I could, so that her two children might learn as much of my native tongue as possible, (she spoke it perfectly). After an hour or so a small town, embellished by an impressive tower of some sort, became visible.

"Yes," the Countess said, "That is Haid, where my family spends the summer; my children are there already, and looking forward to meeting you."

The closer we came to the town, the taller looked the tower, and as we approached it I realized that it was but part of an impressive 5-story castle, laid out in a semi-circle with the tower at one end.

Elizabeth Lloyd-Jones. 1932

103

We pulled up at the gound-floor of the tower; " This is where you are going to live, on the third floor; the butler is on the ground-floor," she said, and led me up a winding staircase to show me my bedroom, which had a window facing the courtyard, and a second door leading into . . . . . *The Tower!*

"This will be <u>your</u> bathroom," she said; "The children and I are next door. Dinner will be in about an hour. I hope you have some evening clothes?" I nearly swooned. Soon I was introduced to the two children; the elder Jack and the younger Osy. They were both nice kids and obviously as shy as I was.

So I changed into my second-best dress, and met the Countess in the corridor. She looked the dress (and my "best" shoes) up and down, and said, "Very nice". (What a relief!) She led me into the dining-room which had a monstrously long table; room for about 25 chairs on either side and one at each end. I was ushered into the middle-chair of one side, with Osy and Jack at my sides, and a very charming gentleman opposite me, who turned out to be Prince Loewenstein, Lord of the castle! But of course, this I did not know; I had imagined that the rather plumpish gentleman at one end of this endless table was the Prince; he sat there, smiling and talking little. But he turned out to be the Prince's Secretary! All this was of course an incredible honor, but from then on I sat near Osy and Jack towards the end of the table. I learned a lot at that table. Everyone had a finger-bowl, and a napkin ring. The ring on the napkin indicated who was to sit where

The view of the Chiemsee from Aisching in South-East Bavaria,
where the Zimmermann family had a summer home.

and was all arranged by the butler. There was a plate before each eater and large dishes of delicious foods were offered from the left and later removed from the right. So all plates were emptied with great cleanliness, everyone having taken just what they wanted.

We retired to the drawing room after dinner, and I gradually steered Osy and Jack off to bed, or, after lunch, for a walk or to beguile ourselves in the garden. This was a large park, with a pond, a rowing boat, and two tennis courts, which the town-folk were permitted to use as a park, so that one was never entirely alone in it.

Osy and Jack and I were permitted to speak ONLY English (at which they were already pretty good), so we took many walks, chattered away in this language, and got along very well. They were at that time about eight and ten, and had ditched their governess for the summer.

Arnold shaving at the boathouse on the Chiemsee.

The day after my arrival, I was staring romantically out of my bed-room window when I heard music coming from somewhere. I looked across the huge courtyard of the castle (104 rooms) and heard little voices and a piano and several familiar classic melodies. The voices turned out to be the two aunts of Osy and Jack, the princesses Resi (Therese) and Maria-Anna. Soon we had made friends, and when I was not occupied with the Eltz children, Maria-Anna and I spent much time together, as we were just the same age. We knitted and practised English and went

shopping in the town, and had a fine old time. I was there for 3 months and was about to leave, (the Eltz family having returned to their Winter Castle) but we had formed such a friendship that the two girls asked me to stay on until the castle was closed for the winter after hunting season.

Summer at the Chiemsee. Yes, Elizabeth knitted her own bathing suit!

105

Arnold, who had taken a summer job at the Pilsen Brewery in Czechoslovakia, was able to come and visit me nearly every weekend. We'd go for walks and generally enjoy the incredibly beautiful area around Haid.

By this time, Arnold and I were definitely "engaged", but a wedding seemed further and further off. Arnold was going through a preparatory period at his uncle Heintz's Spatenbräu Brewery in order to qualify as a brewmaster, and I think that neither of our families were too eager to have us marry foreigners.

Elizabeth and Arnold. c. 1934

I remember well Arnold's first visit to my parents in England in 1930, the Summer after we had first met. We arrived at my parents house in Kenton just before suppertime.

"Wouldn't you like a nice refreshing hot bath before supper ?" my father asked Arnold.

"Yes please," said Arnold, and Pop took him upstairs to show him where the bathroom was.

After one half hour, no Arnold. Three quarters of an hour, still no Arnold.

"I'll go up and see if he's all right," said Pop, only to return in a minute laughing uncontrollably and slapping his thighs. It turned out that he'd found Arnold sitting on the edge of the tub holding the wooden-backed bath thermometer, which we kids had used as a toy boat in our baths for years, trying to translate Fahrenheit into Celsius.

Finally, down he came to supper, which consisted of roast mutton. He received a nice slice and was asked if he would like some mustard.

"Yes please," he said, and helped himself to a goodly portion of Coleman's Mustard. (Quite a different thing from the sweetish, mild Bavarian mustard.)

After taking a generous bite he began fighting for air, with tears streaming down his face!

My parents overlooked both of these episodes, because, after all, he was a foreigner.

So that was our little existence for quite some time: both living in Munich, skiing as and when we could, me knitting, and both working quite hard at the Brewery and the Akademie.

Arnold and Betty's Pop,
unloading the baggage in Kenton.

107

CHAPTER SIX

THE PIE ARE SQUARE SHAWL

Elizabeth wearing the Sawtooth Bordered
Pie Are Square shawl

Shawls ... what a pleasure they are to knit and to wear, and, if it comes to that, how elegant. They use up relatively little wool and are light as a feather. They could be a bore to knit, as they cover such a wide area, but I find myself getting increasingly attached to them the larger they become, and I often add surprisingly wide and/or elaborate borders to prolong their completion.

We hope you will welcome this rather strange addition to your shawl collection. We came up with the name when Meg remembered an old POGO joke;we think it was Howland trying to teach math to Churchy:

Howland: "πr^2"
Churchy: "No, no! Pie are **round**, *cornbread* are square."

So, although this shawl is **round** in the back, and constructed in the same manner as my Pi Shawl *(see Knitter's Almanac or Wool Gathering #1)*, it is **square** in front. We hope you agree that the name is wonderfully silly, but apt.

The original version, which Meg is wearing here, was cast on for travel knitting on a trip to Europe. By the time we arrived at my sister-in-law's house in Bavaria, I had hundreds and hundreds of stitches, and the thing was rather an amorphous mass...she thought I was nuts. By the time we arrived home, and I had finished the entire shawl, I also thought I was nuts! What a peculiar object, even when blocked. I stashed it away in a darkish corner of my wool room among other abandoned projects, and forgot about it.

Years later, during a week of Knitting Camp, Meg asked me to root

Meg wearing the original model.

109

around the house and bring in an assortment of objects for Lace Day, and lo! I found the orphaned shawl, which, for the past several years had been serving as Mouse Motel, and had large brown stains on the back ... "rust-stains" I believe is the euphemism. I brought it in anyway. When we rather shame-facedly displayed the garment, the Knitting Campers did not think I was nuts, they liked it, and begged for instructions.

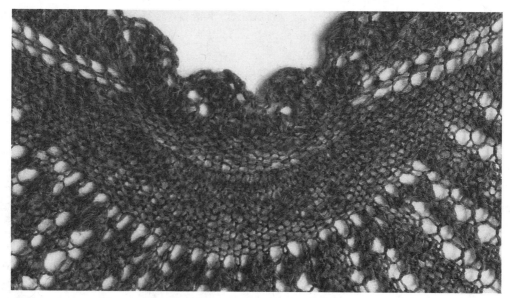

The beginning of the Pie Are Square shawl

EXPOSITION:

This shawl is worked back and forth in garter-stitch. You may insert lace patterns in the main body of the shawl if you wish, and we will give you a choice of two types of border treatments: lace and not lace.

The shawl is begun by casting on enough stitches to go across the back of the neck. Mark the second stitch in from each selvedge. Those marked stitches will be your *diagonal increase points*, where you will increase one stitch each side of the markers every second row.

Work 3 ridges (6 rows) and double the *center* stitches (this does not include the stitches that have resulted from the diagonal increases). Then double the number of ridges, and double the center stitches again, as in the Pi Shawl. Repeat this, always maintaining the diagonal increases, until you have worked a total of four doubling rows.

110

Continue until you think it is long enough (taking into account the fact that, if you are knitting loosely, you will gain considerable length in the blocking). We did not double the number of ridges after the fourth increase.

Select a lace border, and apply to all selvedges and raw stitches. Block. Done.

Now, Dear Un-Sure Knitters:

PIE ARE SQUARE SHAWL

MATERIALS: 12oz Shetland Jumper-weight Wool, *or* 4 3.5oz wheels of 1-ply Icelandic Wool, *or* 8oz Shetland Laceweight Wool (give or take; much depends upon your gauge, the length of the shawl, and the depth of the final border). A 24" circular needle of a size anywhere from a #5-#10.

GAUGE: This will vary. My shawl is knitted in Shetland Jumper-weight Wool. It blocked out at a Gauge of 5 stitches to 1", and is 26" deep at the center back (without the border).
The original shawl *(page 109)* is knitted in Shetland Laceweight Wool at 4.5 stitches to 1", and is 29" long at center back (without border).
Meg's version is in 1-ply Icelandic at a gauge of 3 stitches to 1", and is 33" deep at center back (without border).
So, experiment with wool, needles, and stitch patterns to find a pleasing texture.
CAST ON 20 stitches. Knit 1 ridge (2 rows). Mark stitch #2 and stitch #19 with coilless safety pins.
NOW, every other row. . . Knit to marked stitch, YO (Yarn Over), Knit marked stitch, YO. *(See drawing)*

Repeat this at other end of row, then Knit 1 row plain.

This diagonal increase will continue to the bitter end, unless you choose the round-corner-option (see ahead).

After 3 ridges (6 rows), double the center 16 stitches to 32 by working YO, K1, across them.
Knit 6 more ridges and double the center 32 stitches to 64 by YO, K1 across.
Knit 12 more ridges and double the 64 to 128, still not interrupting the diagonal increasings whose number, by this time, has grown to enormous size.
Knit 24 ridges and double the center 128 to 256 stitches. This will most likely be your final increase - unless you are knitting at a very fine gauge.
Also, you may reach wanted length before you double the final section of ridges.

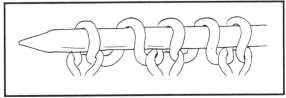

Shows the Yarn Overs each side of the marked stitch

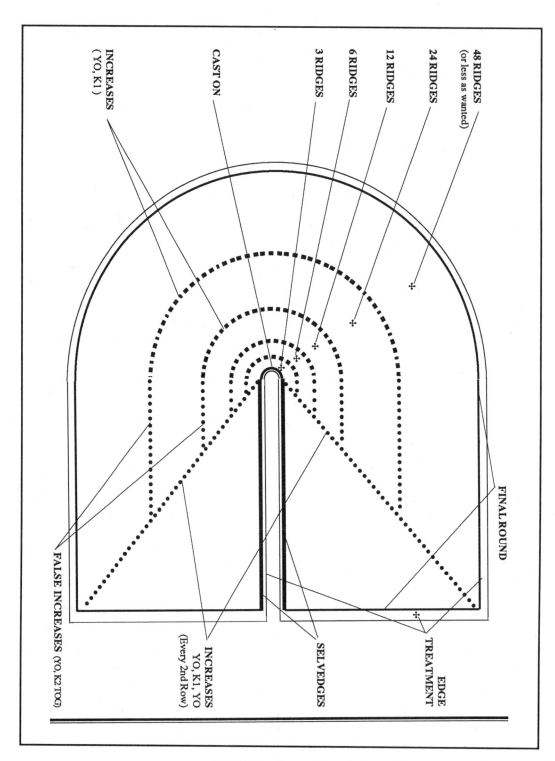

The Pie Are Square Shawl schematic

On my two shawls, I worked 36 more ridges after the last doubling (instead of 48), and Meg's Icelandic shawl has just 20 ridges after the 4th increase...then the border.

Speaking of borders, I'm rather set up with this one:

MY SAWTOOTH BORDER:

This was originally a scalloped edge, but I fussed with it a great deal, and decided that I preferred this sawtoothed edge which is I-Corded as you go.

1. K2, slip 1, K1, psso, K8, turn.
2. Slip 2 purlwise, K6, wool forward (wl fwd), slip 3 purlwise, turn.
3. K2, Sl 1, K1, psso, K7, turn.
4. Sl 2 p'wise, K5, wl fwd, Sl 3 p'wise, turn.
5. K2, Sl 1, K1, psso, K6, turn.
6. Sl 2 p'wise, K4, wl fwd, Sl 3 p'wise, turn.
7. K2, Sl 1, K1, psso, K5, turn.
8. Sl 2 p'wise, K3, wl fwd, Sl 3 p'wise, turn.
9. K2, Sl 1, K1, psso, K4, turn.
10. Sl 2 p'wise, K2, wl fwd, Sl 3 p'wise, turn.
11. K2, Sl 1, K1, psso, K3, turn.
12. Sl 2 p'wise, K1, wl fwd, Sl 3 p'wise, turn.
13. K2, Sl 1, K1, psso, K2, turn.
14. Sl 5 p'wise, turn.
15. K2, Sl 1, K1, psso, K1, turn.
16. Sl 2 p'wise, wl fwd, Sl 2, turn.
17. K2, Sl 1, K1, psso, turn.
18. With left needle, pick up 8 stitches along selvedge PLUS 3 from right needle. Then, with right needle, K2, Sl 1, K1 picked up stitch (a selvedge stitch), psso (3 stitches). Replace the 3 stitches onto left needle .

The "Pie" part of my Pie Are Square Shawl

Now: (K2, Sl 1, K1, psso) 8 times. REPEAT from row one.

If you continue in this mode for the corners, they will be rounded. For sharp 90 degree corners, you would have to figure out a kind of mitre.... you're on your own in this.

After you have bordered the raw stitches, pick up stitches from the selvedges (1 stitch for each garter-stitch ridge), and continue up the front, around the neck, and down the other side. Sew (or Weave) the beginning to the end.

113

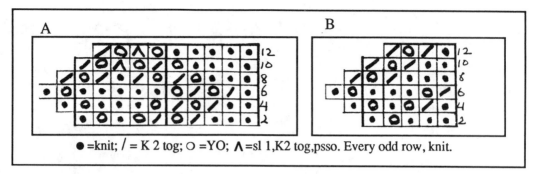

● =knit; / = K 2 tog; ○ =YO; ⋀ =sl 1,K2 tog,psso. Every odd row, knit.

Chart for the borders on the Icelandic Shawl pictured below. Chart A is used around the circle; Chart B is used up the front edges.

Meg's Lace Border was chosen from among 200 lace edgings in that splendid book from Australia: ***CLASSIC KNITTED COTTON EDGINGS*** by Furze Hewitt and Billie Daley; a lifetime's worth of lace edgings.

Beginning at one corner, invisibly cast on the necessary number of stitches for the lace pattern you have chosen.

Work back and forth perpendicular to the raw stitches. Every time you knit back, work the last lace stitch together with one of the un-cast-off-stitches...choosing either K2 tog, or Slip 1, K1, psso, or SSK, or K2 tog through the back loops.

Continue back and forth knitting the lace onto each raw stitch; then up, around, and down the front selvedges. Weave the beginning to the end.

Meg used the 2 patterns shown above, and charted them from the verbal instructions.

Pattern A was a bit too wide for around the neck (it would have folded over), so she altered it slightly for the front edges (pattern B).

*Meg's very warm Icelandic
Pie Are Square Shawl*

114

The border pattern used on the prototype Shetland Laceweight model was taken from Barbara Abbey's wonderful book *KNITTING LACE* (alas, now long out-of-print). Barbara Abbey was a splendid person, and an excellent knitter and writer. Keep your eyes peeled in used bookshops for any of her three books. In addition to the above-mentioned lace book, she wrote *101 WAYS TO IMPROVE YOUR KNITTING* and *THE COMPLETE BOOK OF KNITTING*.

If you have **Knitting Lace**, the border pattern may be found on page 61. But, so the rest of you don't feel too deprived, I will give it to you here.

COCKLESHELL EDGING

18 STITCHES and 16 ROWS, based in Garter-stitch.

Each time you have a" (YO) twice", treat the 2 yarn-overs as 2 separate stitches in the next row.

The opening move to each row: YO, P2 tog, is also called a *fagotting stitch,* and the YO is wrapped all the way around the right needle as you bring the wool forward to P2 tog.

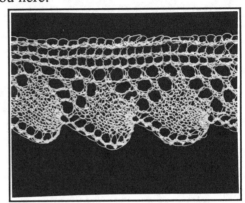

Cockleshell edging

1. YO, P2 tog, (YO, K2 tog) twice, (YO) twice, K2 tog, K8, YO, P2 tog.
2. YO, P2 tog, K10, P1, K6.
3. YO, K2 tog, (YO, K2 tog) twice, K11, YO, P2 tog.
4. YO, P2 tog, K17.
5. YO, P2 tog, (YO, K2 tog) twice, (YO, YO, K2 tog) twice, K7, YO, P2 tog.
6. YO, P2 tog, K9, P1, K2, P1, K6.
7. YO, P2 tog, (YO, K2 tog) twice, K13, YO, P2 tog.
8. YO, P2 tog, K19.
9. YO, P2 tog, (YO, K2 tog) twice, (YO, YO, K2 tog) three times, K7, YO, P2 tog.
10. YO, P2 tog, K9, P1, (K2, P1) twice, K6.
11. YO, P2 tog, (YO, K2 tog) twice, K16, YO, P2 tog.
12. YO, P2 tog, K22.
13. YO, P2 tog, (YO, K2 tog) twice, (YO, YO, K2 tog) four times, K8, YO, P2 tog.
14. YO, P2 tog, K10, P1, (K2, P1) three times, K6.
15. YO, P2 tog, (YO, K2 tog) twice, K20, YO, P2 tog.
16. K2 tog, K9, pull 9 over the last stitch just knitted on the righthand needle.

Return to row one, and repeat.

115

Meg and I have done a bit of playing around with the original instructions, and offer you the following options. Look them over before you begin your shawl, and perhaps opt for one or two of them.

OPTION #1: The YO, K1 increases produce a nice row of decorative holes. They stop suddenly where the diagonal section begins. To continue the chain un-broken you may work FAKE HOLES by YO, K2 tog before and after the actual YO, K1 increases. You may stop the fake holes at the diagonal increases, or continue them all the way to the front selvedges.

OPTION #2: The diagonal increases cause the front corners to hang (droop) lower than the rest of the shawl. Meg obviated this by discontinuing the diagonal increases about 4-5" from the lower edge of the shawl, BUT continued the decorative appearance of the holes by working K2 tog, YO, K1, YO, SSK at each diagonal corner. This cessation of increasing will *round* the front corners.

OPTION #3: Not only do the corners hang a bit low, but the rounded back seems a bit short by comparison. If you knit loosely (as in the Icelandic shawl), the back can be blocked longer. Otherwise, consider augmenting the back length by incorporating an occasional Short Row or two in the sections between the increase rows.

OPTION #4: I kept my shawl entirely in Garter-Stitch (my fave). Meg chose to insert lace patterns in the sections between the increase rows. You may make it all lace, or knit only the round (π) back section in lace. Or, as Meg did, work lace up to the diagonals, and keep the front triangles in garter-stitch. Meg was in a hurry to meet the photo deadline and did not pin out her lace border. After seeing the photos, she was sorry, and has since re-blocked the shawl with the borders sharply pinned out into scallops, making them much more defined and lacy.

Instructions for the lace border on the original "mouse" shawl were taken from a long-out-of-print book. However, a close version may now be found in the Australian book, *Classic Knitted Cotton Edgings*.

The lace patterns shown here were both taken from the Barbara Walker *Treasury Of Knitting Patterns* series. All of

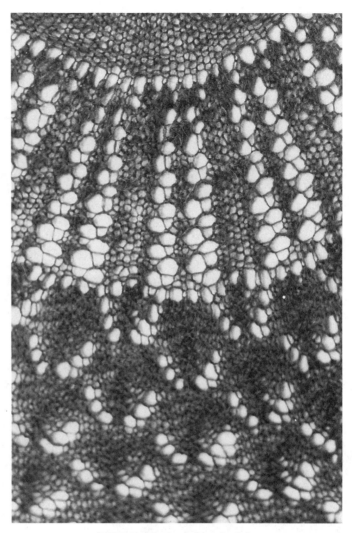

Filling in the round back of the shawl with lace patterns.

Barbara Walker's books are highly recommended, which reminds me: I hope that you have a largish supply of stitch-pattern books on your knitting shelf, enabling you to pick and choose a lace or texture stitch for whatever garment you are knitting.

We now consider the Pi Shawl squared away...

Elizabeth's pencil sketch of Mill Bluff, Wisconsin. Spring 1972.

118

. . .Digressions

Today is the blizzard of '61. I have never seen the white stuff come down so fast and so suddenly. Up until now, this has been Milwaukee's most snowless winter. The schoolhouse had a few measly inches, but the city has been bare except for an extremely sparse White Christmas. Actually, it's worked out quite nicely as this is the winter when Arnold and I formally gave up downhill skiing. After all, at fifty, every time I contemplate a timid turn it flashes before my mind's eye: what of my femur, my pelvis, my poor old brittle ankles. . . .and that is no state of mind in which to ski. Anyway, I've had a good thirty years of it, and Arnold even longer.

Skiing has always meant a great deal to Arnold and me - after all, we did a lot of our courting under ideal snow-conditions. So it seemed only fair to initiate the children, come what might, in this form of family agony. . . the marshalling of ten each of skis, poles, and boots. And ten warm slippers for the trip home, not to mention about 30 mittens - oh well, you know it yourselves. Also the snow here in Wisconsin is rarely even approximately ideal, vacillating between murderous ice and mud-sherbet.

I will now meander back to the good old days and describe a weekend's skiing in Munich in the thirties. You got up at about 2 A.M. During Carnival you didn't even bother to go to bed at all - just went home to change your artistic costume for ancient ski-pants, venerable boots, a waterproof parka if you were lucky, and a cav-ernous rucksack. Skis were wooden with no metal edges, and poles shoulder-high and made of bam-boo. Get this: you probably *walked* to the railroad station. Perhaps trams were rare at this hour of the morning, but a part of the moti-vation for this trek was a glad-ness to be able to save the 20

Bavarian Valley c. 1930

119

pfennig fare. After all you could get a beer for 20 pfennig, or even for 10. It seems to me in memory to have been generally about an hour's walk from Schwabing to the station, so you shouldered your skis and off you set.

From time to time as you tramped along, you would hear the clatter of other heavy boots coming out of the side-streets, all skiers converging on the station, until there was a steady flow in this direction. During Carnival there was of course a counter-flow of home-bound revellers, and rude and derogatory banter would be exchanged, each party despising the folly of the other. The station was a veritable forest of skis through which you had to struggle to find your friends and cronies. Then on to the platform to wait for the train, and more struggle to get a good seat and be more or less all together. The technique was to leave one or two buddies on the platform while the others went in to secure seats. Then the window was opened, skis passed through and stowed on the racks inside the compartment. All hands usually settled down for a long winter's nap for two or three hours until the train reached the mountains. The last stop was Bayerisch Zell on our favourite train, but for several stops before this the passengers would thin out. Bayerisch Zell was not perhaps the best ski-stop, but they who got out last got in first for the return trip, and had best choice of seats.

Alpine Mountain Village.

I suppose I shall never forget the very first trip. I had been sound asleep, and somewhere - Fischhausen-Neuhaus I think - I suddenly awoke. It had become broad daylight during my slumber, and there was brilliant snow, clean, and actually sparkling. I had never seen snow sparkle before. The English stuff was mostly white, but soggy, and I suddenly realized that all the stories of the clean, crisp shining snow in the Bavarian Alps had been true. It started a train of intoxication in me which had the most far-reaching consequences, and brought me the best things in life; can you wonder that I want to pass this sentiment on to our children?

So out of the train into the powdery creaking stuff, shoulder the skis, and off up the mountain. To begin with it would be icy-cold, with your nostrils sticking together and your eyes watering. But the higher the skiers climbed the mountain, the higher the sun climbed the sky, and by the top you had shed everything you could, and the rucksack was nearly cutting your shoulders off. That is, you didn't of course go right to the top - there was always some kind of stopping-place, with a Wirtshaus or ski-huette, supplied with beer, milk, and yellow pea-soup.

Out of the rucksacks came black bread, har-boil-deggs, and wurst. Such guzzling, I can taste it now. Skiing went on all day; climb up, zoom down, climb up, zoom down. All kinds and descriptions of skiers, none of them too terribly good by present standards, and some of them

Alpine Wurzhütte

pitifully awkward. I wasn't too bad, and finally with much effort became a tolerable companion on the mountain. Arnold was always among the good ones. But skiing was different in those days. It demanded more endurance and less dash, and was to my mind infinitely more rewarding - more like winter mountaineering. Climbing was a long slow process, and of course important to learn and practice properly. It had quite definite techniques, and a poor climber just got left more and more behind, until the others were way out of sight. Then he would round a corner and find them waiting there for him, impatiently tapping their skis. He would reach them, puffing and blowing, and completely pooped, and without a second's pause they would all set off again, nicely refreshed by their wait, while the poor slow one had no wait at all. I believe the theory was that it was bad for the learner to stop anywhere; his muscles tightened, or loosened, or something.

Betty, having a little something on the mountain.

By the same token it was absolutely and rigidly forbidden for the pitiful novice to let so much as a drop of liquid pass his lips until he reached the summit. He occasionally passed enticing little springs gushing out of the mountainside through iron pipes into little troughs. No. Or he would come upon groups of actually *resting* skiers, whose wives and girlfriends were allowed to take nips of cold tea. No. Please, just a handful of snow? No, most certainly not. Do you want to kill yourself? He was only permitted to nibble on

121

dried apricots, if he had had the forethought to provide himself with these. An advantage of being the slow one trailing behind was that one could sneak surreptitious icicles to suck on. This was supposed to be certain death, preceded by agonizing colic, but it certainly never hurt me. So you see, Nature takes care of her own.

The climb up the Alpspitze.

Exhausting or no, the climb was certainly one of the best parts of a very good sport. To anyone who knows the mountains in winter, I do not have to describe it. To those who don't, it is almost useless. The trek begins in deep, icy-blue shadow, looking up to the sunlit peaks; through the villages to the jingle of sleighbells as the country people go about their business. Then through the outskirts of summer chalets, mostly shuttered, and mostly called by girl's

Arnold and Elizabeth

names - Villa Charlotte, Villa Kunigunde, imagine - then the road would narrow, pass through a gate and start uphill. First between snowy meadows with scattered farmhouses - house and barn both in one long building (so that the cows would keep the people warm), and hay-barns. Then the forests would start, and the track would become a Ziehweg, that is, hollowed out like half a tube from having logs dragged down along it.

The sun on the peaks would become more and more and nearer and nearer, until at last you were actually in it. Sometimes here, five minutes rest was allowed. Bliss. And so on up to the goal of beer or milk, and soup, through the checkered sunlight of the forests, where the trees would sometimes smell of warm pitch in the sun, and at last on the slopes themselves where the track wound through a scattering of people who had come up by an even earlier train.

The reward.

If you were lucky enough to have two days off, and could afford it, you spent the night in the hut, on the Matratzenlager: a row of hard mattresses and cold army blankets. This couldn't have mattered less; you were out like a light, slept like a log, and were awoken good and early for some kind of breakfast and then more skiing.

Arnold belonged to the Alpenverein, which meant that we could use their huts for very little money, and cook our own breakfasts etc. This didn't help me any because I couldn't cook. On one embarassing occasion some kind people, having made themselves an enormous supper of Kaiserschmarren, and having some batter left over, asked if we would like it. To be just to myself, I had never eaten Schmarren and didn't even know what it looked like. So I poured that

damned batter into a saucepan without butter or anything, and expected it to cook. Nobody said anything, and I didn't know enough German to understand the subsequent muttered remarks, but I knew enough to understand that they were derogatory.

It was on trips like these that we learned to appreciate the true value of porridge, of which I had had too much as a child and couldn't stand. But when I saw how light it was to carry up the mountain, how sustaining, and above all how cheap, I damned well learned to stand it. And I'm pretty sure my children (the girls, that is; Tom is very sensible about porridge) will go through the same process.

Poor things, they certainly were stuffed on it as children, but I was convinced then, and still am, that it is

Sun trap.

123

the very best form of food for children, and one should get as much as possible into them before they get wise to it. They had it in bread, soup, cookies, and even pudding, for which I would sweeten it up, and let it set.

At breakfast, it was, "Now eat up your nice porridge, and if you are good, you may have *sugar* on the *second* plateful." And how smart of me to call it that. On comparing notes in school, they surely had no inkling that what they were knocking back every morning were plates full of the notorious "oatmeal". So I fooled them for at least six years, and I am convinced gave them a foundation of good health that is standing them in magnificent stead. I never saw a healthier gang.

Well, porridge was a standby for trips where everything had to be carried on one's own back, along with tea, dried soups, hard sausage, and eggs. Rather like camping now. Dried food with the addition of melted snow (or lake water, as the case may be) can be very sustaining, and to hell with fresh green and yellow vegetables and refrigeration. At least we didn't suffer from lack of energy on our ski-trips.

As Sunday began to wear on into afternoon, we would collect our parts and attachments, ski down the mountain, take perhaps a quick beer or milk in Gasthaus Terofal while waiting for the train, fight for places in said train, and sleep all the way home.

Funny about milk, too. It was the very first thing Arnold and I had a small fight about. I wanted milk, and he said no, beer. I said milk was better for you, and he said, actually, no, beer had more nourishment. I was absolutely staggered. This was the first time he had come out with one of his famous bald-faced lies, in such a convincing and selbstverstandlich (see what I mean about German) manner that one doubts the evidence of one's own logic, information and proof.

I am used to it now, and can nearly always giggle, but at first it frustrated me to the point of frenzy. As a very simplified and primitive example, he said the other day, "This is birch-wood," and I said, "No, ash," and he said, "That's what I said, ash." I mean, what can one do in a case like that? And he does it all the time, let alone when the point in question goes back a month or so. I can't possibly keep tape-recordings of everything we have ever said, but that would be the only way to refute him. And of course I don't count his saying that I had never told him some-thing when he had been hearing me at the time, but not *listening*. Oh well. He's a good old man, and I have developed methods of irritating him right back, if I wish to employ them.

This has brought us a long way from skiing, but this vein shall be returned to and at length, I'm sure. I don't call these my digressions for nothing.

Arnold
and
Elizabeth

125

Cully wearing the Norwegian Pullover

CHAPTER SEVEN

A NORWEGIAN PULLOVER

It was back in 1955 that I first sold one of my designs to a magazine; a Norwegian Pullover - two of them actually - and I can see them now. One I had made for Meg in natural oatmeal Sheepswool with a cream pattern, and a dark brown trim. The other was pale grey, with patterns in cream and charcoal, and a dashing scarlet trim. They both had zippers along one shoulder to facilitate getting them off and on.

The first authentic Norwegian Drop-Shouldered sweater I ever met was given to me to mend, and I was bowled over when I found the machine stitching and the cut edges. What an uncomplicated, clean, simply-shaped garment - not to mention pleasant to knit and comfortable to wear.

This classic sweater is one of the most basic of all methods of circular garment construction. It consists of a large tube for the body and two smaller, shaped tubes for the sleeves. The body is knitted from the lower edge to the shulders without a thought for armhole shaping. The sleeves are then knitted from the cuff up (so the stitches of the color-pattern will be the right way up, and match the body). When all three pieces are finished, the sleeve tops are carefully measured against the sides of the body. The depth of the armhole is marked on the body with a basting thread. One (or two) rows of machine stitching - using a small stitch and a loose tension - are run down one side of the basting, across the bottom, and up the other side. Cut on the basting. Sew (or weave) the shoulders to complete the circle of the armhole. Sew in the sleeves from the right side. Finish off the neck stitches in any of a number of ways *(see ahead)*, and you are done.

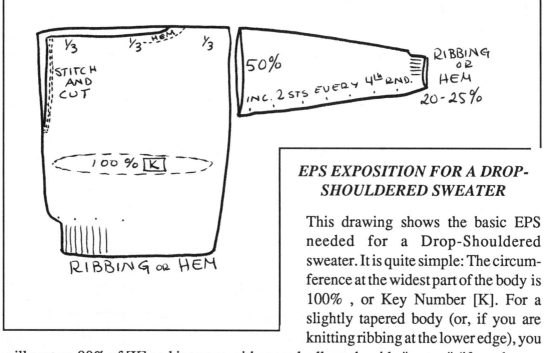

Labels in drawing:
⅓ ⅓--HEM. ⅓
STITCH AND CUT
50%
INC. 2 STS EVERY 4ᵗʰ RND.
RIBBING OR HEM 20-25%
100% [K]
RIBBING OR HEM

EPS EXPOSITION FOR A DROP-SHOULDERED SWEATER

This drawing shows the basic EPS needed for a Drop-Shouldered sweater. It is quite simple: The circumference at the widest part of the body is 100% , or Key Number [K]. For a slightly tapered body (or, if you are knitting ribbing at the lower edge), you will cast on 90% of [K] and increase, either gradually at the side "seams" (if you have a hem at the lower edge), OR increase the whole 10% in the first stocking stitch round above the ribbing. The cuff is about 20-25% [K], and you shape the sleeve by increasing two stitches every 4th (or 5th) round until the sleeve width is nearly 50% of [K]. This wide sleeve was the proportion used in the old, traditional garments; you may want to reduce it to 40-45%. The neck opening is approximately 33-40% of the body width, depending upon which neck treatment you choose.

We will give you a more detailed schematic for Cully's Norwegian Pullover in a few pages. You may like to knit straight from the drawing. If that prospect sounds daunting, here are more familiar verbal instructions. We will give the numbers specific to Cully's actual sweater; make your necessary alterations by working with EPS and your calculator.

CULLY'S NORWEGIAN PULLOVER

SIZE: 43" around widest part of body.

MATERIALS: 5 4oz skeins 2-ply natural undyed "blacksheep" Sheepswool, 3 skeins of natural cream Sheepswool, 1oz Heather Shetland Wool used doubled. A 16" and 24" circular needle of a size to give you the wanted gauge (approx. #5-6); a 24"needle a size or two smaller for body ribbing; a smaller size d.p. needles for cuffs.

STITCH GAUGE: 4.5 stitches to 1".

ROW GAUGE: 6.75 rows to 1". *(This is one of the few instances where Row Gauge is necessary, as you have to know how deep* the chest patterns will be...and where to begin them so that they fit into the wanted length of the body.)

KEY NUMBER [K]: 43" x 4.5 = 194, which we're changing to **196** so as to be divisible by 4 to fit the "lice" in evenly. *(The original Norwegian jackets of this type were called 'Luskofte' - translation: Lice Jacket! And I had always thought, romantically, that 'lus' meant little 'lights'. Nothing of the kind!)*

BODY: With a 24" needle 1 or 2 sizes smaller, **CAST ON 174** (90% [K]), and work K1B, P1 for 2-3", or wanted height of ribbing. *(Insert a Short Row across the back of the ribbing, if wanted, as you cannot fit them into the body without lousing up your lice.)*
Increase to 196 [K] in first stocking stitch round by K8, M1 around. Knit 2 rounds *(inserting a 2nd Short Row, if wanted).*

Establish "lice" as follows: Join in Cream wool, and work **K3 blacksheep, K1 cream,** around. Now work 3 (or 4) rounds plain. *(The traditional distance between 'lice' is 3 stitches and 3 rows, or 5 stitches*

and 5 rows. *We will vary that slightly by working the lice 3 stitches, but 4 rows apart ... making them more equidistant.)*

At 10.5 - 11" from wanted total body length, begin color patterns below. Remember to carry the pattern color loosely across the back of the work.

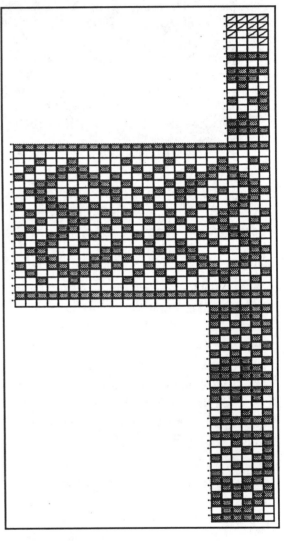

Read chart from right to left; bottom to top. The dot at the end of each line ="repeat". The diagonal lines at the top are for the third color trim. Note that the colors are reversed for the main pattern.

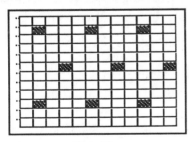

Lice Chart

129

*Elizabeth and Meg, knitting.
Wisconsin , c. 1949*

Be sure to balance the patterns evenly, first deciding whether you want the center of the garment to fall *between* the patterns, or in the *middle* of one of them.

BALANCE: Leave a "seam" stitch at each side; count the remaining stitches on the front; divide that number by the number of stitches in the pattern you will be using, and whatever is left over, divide evenly between the beginning and the end.

OR: beginning at center-front stitch, count backwards in increments of the pattern repeat. When you reach the side "seam" stitch - wherever you are on the pattern - that is where you will begin each round.

You may sneak in another Short Row across the back in the trim color. **Put all body stitches on a piece of wool.**

SLEEVE:

With 4 double-pointed needles, **CAST ON** 38 sts (25% [K]). Work K1b, P1b for 3-4".

OPTION: If you want the cuff to be reversible when it is turned back, the K1b, P1b is necessary. However, P1b is quite laborious, and we have been known to cheat a bit by working it only to the halfway point, then finishing the cuff in good old K1b, P1.

The cuff is "bloused" slightly, by increasing to 50 stitches **(K3, M1 around)** in the first stocking stitch round. Begin the "lice". After a few inches, establish regular increases as follows:

Mark the center "seam" stitch, and keep it in background color throughout. Increase 1 stitch each side of the marked stitch every 5th round until you have 96-98 stitches,

130

*Meg and Elizabeth, **Knitting Around** together on the same piece of knitting: the body of Cully's Norwegian Pullover. Meg is wearing a cardigan version of the same sweater; Elizabeth is wearing the Bog Jacket.*

(50% [K]). Work straight to wanted sleeve length.

To calculate proper sleeve length for this dropped-shoulder style, measure a favorite-fitting garment from the center of the neck back to the cuff. Now measure half the width of the finished body. Subtract the small number from the large, and the result is the wanted sleeve length.

We worked two different sleeve-top treatments:
In the photo here, the sleeve on the left is cast off in the usual manner; the sleeve on the right has an added built-in facing, typical of real Norwegian

garments. To work the facing, complete the sleeve to wanted length, but do not cast off. Instead, switch to a lighter weight wool, and loosely knit around for a good inch. Cast off loosely. This facing will later be sewn down over the cut edge of the armhole.

CULLY'S NORWEGIAN SWEATER

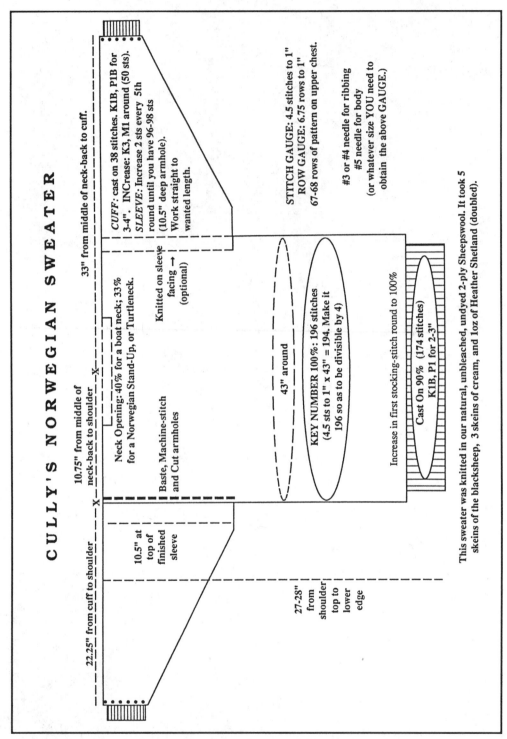

CUFF: cast on 38 stitches. K1B, P1B for 3-4". INCrease: K3, M1 around (50 sts). SLEEVE: Increase 2 sts every 5th round until you have 96-98 sts (10.5" deep armhole). Work straight to wanted length.

Knitted on sleeve facing → (optional)

33" from middle of neck-back to cuff.

10.75" from middle of neck-back to shoulder

Neck Opening: 40% for a boat neck; 33% for a Norwegian Stand-Up, or Turtleneck.

Baste, Machine-stitch and Cut armholes

STITCH GAUGE: 4.5 stitches to 1"
ROW GAUGE: 6.75 rows to 1"
67-68 rows of pattern on upper chest.

#3 or #4 needle for ribbing
#5 needle for body
(or whatever size YOU need to obtain the above GAUGE.)

43" around

KEY NUMBER 100%: 196 stitches
(4.5 sts to 1" x 43" = 194. Make it 196 so as to be divisible by 4)

Increase in first stocking-stitch round to 100%

Cast On 90% (174 stitches)
K1B, P1 for 2-3"

22.25" from cuff to shoulder

10.5" at top of finished sleeve

27-28" from shoulder top to lower edge

This sweater was knitted in our natural, unbleached, undyed 2-ply Sheepswool. It took 5 skeins of the blacksheep, 3 skeins of cream, and 1oz of Heather Shetland (doubled).

The schematic for Cully's Norwegian Pullover.

ASSEMBLY:

Carefully measure the top of a finished sleeve against the side of the finished body.

Mark where the bottom of the sleeve hits the body. Run a basting thread (wool) from the top of the body to the marker, being sure to stay in the side "seam" stitch.

With a small stitch, and loose tension, machine stitch down the side of the basting, across the bottom, and up the other side. Stay close to the basting thread.

Repeat on other side.

Cut on the basting. The armhole will appear to stretch; not to worry, you measured carefully. It is the nature of knitted stitches to expand upon being cut.

Before you sew the sleeves in, you must complete the circle of the armhole by sewing up the shoulders. We do not recommend weaving, as the weight of the voluminous sleeves may stretch the shoulders. You may *cast off* the body stitches, and sew the edges together; or cast them off together from the inside. For 3-Needle I-Cord Cast Off, see ahead.

Pin the top of the sleeve to the top of the shoulder; the bottom to the bottom. Pin again at the quarter points, and the eighths as well.

Select a vertical row on the body into which you will be sewing, (one or two rows away

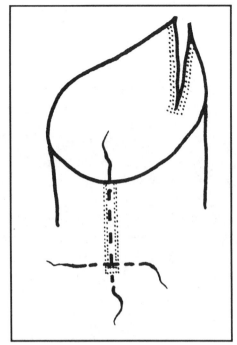

After the cut.

from the machine stitching), and do not veer from that row as you sew.

Sew the sleeves in from the right side - going in-and-out of a stitch on the sleeve, then in-and-out of a chunk of the body.
OPTION: If you want to take the time, you MAY count the stitches to rows. Since there is a 5:7 ratio, you will work (stitches to rows) *1:1, 1:2, 1:1, 1:2, 1:1. Repeat from *.
We don't do that, as we find the empirical method more satisfactory.

Now you will have to decide upon a neck treatment, as that will determine what percentage of the shoulders you will sew together.

133

STAND-UP COLLAR:

Sew up 1/3 of the top of the body for each shoulder. With a 16" needle, pick up the stitches of the remaining 1/3, and knit around to wanted height. Purl 1 round, and work a hem in lighter-weight wool. Do Not Cast Off, but sew the stitches down right off the needle in order to maintain elasticity. If you do not have lighter wool for the hem, decrease 10% of the stitches one round after the purl round.

Stand-Up Collar

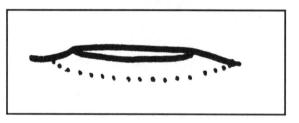

Flat Hem

BOATNECK WITH FLAT HEM:

Sew up about 1/5 (20%) for each shoulder, leaving 40% for the neck opening. Pick up all the neck stitches, and Purl one round. Change to lighter-weight wool, and knit the hem. To provide sufficient fabric for the hem to lie nice and flat at those sharp 180° corners, you must increase like mad: Mark the 3 corner stitches at each end, M1, K3, M1 at each corner *every* round. When the hem is deep enough (1.5 to 2"), do not cast off, but sew stitches down right off the needle.

NORWEGIAN NECK:

Sew up about 1/3 of each shoulder. Pick up the stitches across the back of the neck only. Knit back and forth in garter-stitch for about 2". Cast off. Fold the sides of the garter-stitch piece to the front corners of the neck opening, and sew them down. For the raw front stitches: you may simply cast them off, or hem them.

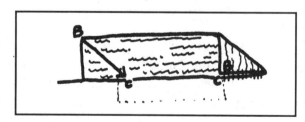

Norwegian Garter-Stitch Neck.

TURTLE NECK:

Sew up about 1/3 for each shoulder. Pick up all neck stitches, and work K2, P2 to the point of exhaustion: about 7-9" worth. Cast off very loosely. *(I have been known to insert a sneaky increase in the last ribbed round to assure that the cast off edge will go over the wearer's head with relative ease.)*

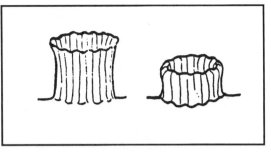

Turtle neck; up or down.

I-Corded neck and shoulders.

BOATNECK USING 3-NEEDLE I-CORD CAST OFF FOR NECK AND SHOULDERS :

This will unite the shoulders, cast them off, and I-Cord them all at once.

Allow about 40% for the neck opening.

Beginning at one shoulder, put the front body stitches on one needle; the back stitches on a second needle. Work from the right side.

With a third needle, **CAST ON 3** (I-Cord) stitches. Immediately transfer them to one of the two shoulder needles, and *K2 of the I-Cord stitches, **Slip 1, K2 stitches together** (one from the front; one from the back needle), **PSSO**. Replace 3 stitches onto one of the shoulder needles. Repeat from *.

After an inch or so, take a jaundiced look at the I-Cord: is it pulling up? is it sagging? If so, adjust your needle size up or down accordingly.

Continue to the neck opening, and work I-Cord Cast Off across the front of the neck, with just 2 needles. At the other side of the neck opening, resume the 3-Needle cast off across the other shoulder.

All that remains is to work I-Cord Cast Off across the back of the neck, skillfully weaving in the beginning and the end of the I-Cord. (See the accompanying video for great detail on this technique.)

Generally speaking, a single application of I-Cord is an insufficient border for stocking-stitch, as, over a longish distance, it will not prevent the natural curl inherent in stocking stitch. However, in our experience, it will work over a *short* distance, such as the above neck, the cuff edge of a mitten, or the armholes of a vest. For multiple I-Cord, see ahead.

135

OTHER OPTIONS

HEMS:

On a loosely-fitting garment such as this sweater, a hem can be a handsome alternative to ribbing at the lower edge and the cuffs.

Hems should be added at the very end to enable you to sew down the raw stitches on the inside of the body, maintaining the elasticity of the fabric. If you cast on for the hem, it will produce a tight, unyielding edge, which may cause an unsightly indentation to show on the right side.

To plan ahead for hems, use Long-Tail Casting On for beginning body and sleeves (also called Two Strand). This yields a neat Outline-Stitch side, and a Purl-bump side. Make sure the Outline-Stitch is the Right side, and continue up the body, (or sleeves).

When the three tubes are completed, *then* add the hems.

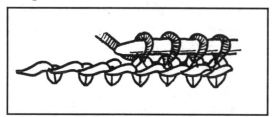

Knitting up behind the Outline-Stitch

From the right side, knit up into the Purl-Bumps *behind* the Outline-Stitch of the cast on edge, *(see drawing)*. Work one round on all stitches. Next round: decrease 10% (K8, K2 tog around) to "hold in".

OPTION: If you work the hems in a lighter-weight wool, the 10% decrease may be omitted.

Work the hem to wanted depth (2-3"), knitting in names, dates, or secret messages that only the wearer will know. This always brings up the problem of which way up to knit the message. Should it be legible to the wearers when they flip their hem up to read it ? Or should the wearers be able to flash the message at passers-by?

At wanted depth, do not cast off, but turn the hem to the inside...aha! You see how nicely the hem folds along the Outline-Stitch edge? It makes a good substitute for the traditional "Purl One Round". Now simply slide 10-15 stitches at a time off the needle, and, with a sharp sewing-up needle, skim each stitch down to the inside of the garment.

NEATEN CUT ARMHOLE EDGES:

If you decided not to knit in the facing at the top of the sleeve, you may now neaten the cut edge as follows:

With a steam iron, puff at the cut edge, and cause it to fold *toward* the sleeve (it will resist, but bend it to your will).

Tack the edge in place, using Herringbone embroidery stitch.

FOR A CARDIGAN:

If you have decided upon a cardigan in advance, cast on an additional 3-5 stitches at the center front as a field for the machine-stitching and cutting to come. In a patterned sweater, such as this, keep the center stitches in background color, and every few rounds, anchor the carried color in the very center stitch. This will serve as a knitted-in basting thread, and will save you that step later on.

At 2-3" shy of wanted body length, make a Kangaroo Pouch for a square neck:

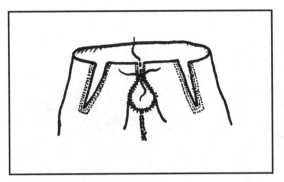

Armholes have been stitched and cut; Kangaroo Pouch and center-front have been stitched, and are about to be cut.

This rather peculiar pouch will lower the neck front, and will save you from having to Cut Out and Throw Away an actual piece of knitting.

Put 6-7" worth of stitches (27 - 31 stitches) on a piece of wool at the center front. **CAST ON** 3 - 5 stitches in their place (use the same number that you have for the cardigan front), and continue **knitting around** to wanted length of body from lower edge to shoulder.

Baste and machine stitch the Kangaroo Pouch; then the center front.

Cut.

KNITTED-ON BORDERS

GARTER-STITCH BORDER:
Begin at the lower right corner with the right side facing you. The border will be knitted perpendicular to the body, and, after years of trial and error, the following ratio made itself known to me:

Knit up 2 stitches for every 3 rounds. In other words, knit up into rounds #1 and 2, skip 3, knit up 4 and 5, skip 6, etc. This will give you 1/3 fewer stitches in the border than there are rounds in the body, and seems to be just right for garter-stitch on stocking-stitch.

Continue up to the top of the right front.

Now, along the horizontal bit, knit up *all* stitches. (They will be waiting on the piece of wool.)

Knit up 2 for 3 along the short vertical piece to the neck back.

Knit up *all* stitches across the back of the neck, and repeat (in reverse) for the left side.

Work back and forth on all front and neck stitches, mitering the corners as follows:

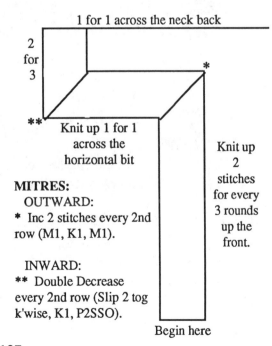

1 for 1 across the neck back

2 for 3

*

**

Knit up 1 for 1 across the horizontal bit

Knit up 2 stitches for every 3 rounds up the front.

MITRES:
  OUTWARD:
* Inc 2 stitches every 2nd row (M1, K1, M1).

  INWARD:
** Double Decrease every 2nd row (Slip 2 tog k'wise, K1, P2SSO).

Begin here

Elizabeth and Meg, during a weekend family camping trip, c. 1949. Note Meg's Norwegian sweater, dashing socks, and petulant expression.

OUTWARD MITRE:

This is worked at the two top front corners. Mark the corner stitch with a safety pin.

On the right side: knit to the marked stitch, M1, K marked stitch, M1 (working the M1s in opposing directions if wanted...picky-picky.) And, to keep a neat diagonal stocking stitch at the corner:

On the wrong side, purl the marked stitch.

INWARD MITRE:

These are worked at the inner corners, and produce a nice, square neckline. Mark the corner stitch with a safety pin.

On the right side: work a double decrease as follows: Knit to within one stitch of the marked stitch. Slip 2 stitches together knitwise, K1, pass the 2 slipped stitches over.

On the wrong side, purl the marked stitch.

If you would rather have **ROUNDED INNER CORNERS**, you would put 6 fewer stitches on the Kangaroo Pouch thread, and decrease one stitch at each end of the threaded stitches for three rounds. Then, as you work the border, ignore the Inward Mitre.

NECK-BACK SHAPING

This is necessary to cause the back border to conform to the wearer's neck (otherwise, it would stick straight up in a "flower pot" mode).

After 2 or 3 ridges, decrease quite sharply across the neck-back only: K3, K2 tog, from shoulder point to shoulder point.

Choose your favorite buttonhole, and knit them in, evenly spaced, after 3 ridges.

Cully in his Norwegian Pullover.

Work another 3 or 4 ridges, and **CAST OFF** loosely, in purl, on the right side. Or, for the best cast off on garter stitch, work **Sewn Casting Off.** *(see appendix)*

MULTIPLE I-CORD BORDER

(See close-up photo of "3&1" cardigan in the color section, and on the next page.)

A **single** application of I-Cord at the selvedge of stocking stitch is insufficient to prevent the stocking stitch from curling. However, a **double** application of I-Cord works quite well, and a **triple** application does the job admirably.

Starting at the lower corner, a row or two beyond the machine stitching, from the wrong side, with a smaller size needle, pick up body stitches to be I-Corded.

You alone will determine the amount of stitches you pick up, as there are too many variables for us to dictate a specific ratio: are you using a different type of wool? What size needle are you working with? Are you knitting into the front or the back of the stitch? You may pick up 1 stitch for every row, or 4 stitches for every 5 rows, or 9 for 10. Experiment. After a few inches, take a narrow look at it. If the I-Cord is sagging, or pulling up too tightly, adjust your needle size accordingly.

With the ratio established, I-Cord your way around the border, turning corners as described in Chapters Four and Five.

Finish off by drawing the working wool through the 3 stitches, pulling them closed, and darning in the end.

The second application is easier, because the ratio has already been determined, so now you simply knit up 1 stitch for each row(let) of the existing I-Cord. Be sure to stay in the same vertical row all the way around.

During the second application, you may want to install **I-CORD BUTTON-HOLES** - either Hidden or Looped. See Chapter Four for both of these.

The third row of I-Cord may be used to secure the Looped Buttonholes: give the loop a twist, and knit the third I-Cord into the twist, which will hold it in place.

We stopped at three layers, using three different colors, but there is no reason why you may not continue - knitting a rainbow I-Cord border as wide as you like.

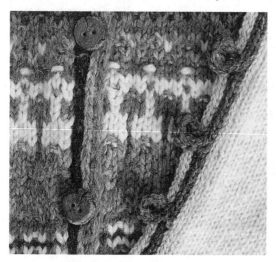

Close-up of Triple I-Cord Borders with Looped or Hidden Buttonholes. The 3&1 design is a lovely, rhythmical pattern to knit: always 3 stitches of one color, 1 stitch of another. The dash (-) through some of the stitches on the chart opposite, are occasional purl stitches, and enrich an already beautiful color-pattern.

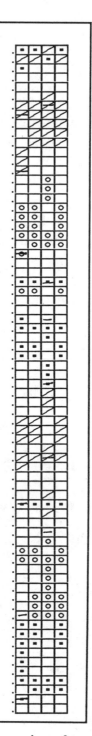

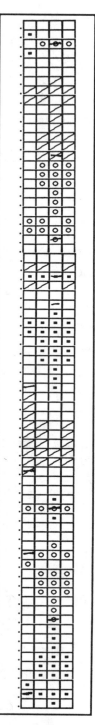

...continue from here   begin here...

Chart for the "3&1" sweater shown in the color section.

140

. . . Digressions

Times were tough in Germany in 1936. Arnold had been unable to get a job as a brewmaster or even assistant brewmaster, and was working as a journeyman brewer in a small, tucked-away brewery in Palling, East of the Chiemsee in Bavaria.

We had been engaged for six years, and still he insisted it was unthinkable to get married with him holding only a temporary, low paying job. Finally, I couldn't take it anymore, so I left for England and soon found a job, through my art school chum Peggy Collier, as an English-speaking companion in the family of Baron von Koskull in Kuusankoski, Finland.

I took a London train to the eastcoast town of Hull, where I boarded a Finnish

The Chiemsee from Arnold's boathouse, with the Fraueninsel in shadow.

freighter to Kotka on the Finnish South coast. The whole Koskull family waited for me in a big American family car. We drove to Kuusankoski, where the Baron was a bigshot in the local papermill, and just travelling through the countryside was an experience in itself. We passed red, wooden barns and low, red, wooden houses. The terrain was flat to slightly rolling with mixed woods of spruce and birch; remarkably like central Wisconsin, although then, of course, I didn't know this. We came past vast moors and travelled intermittantly on solid granite rock, which the

The Baron von Koskull, his family, and friends

141

Finns incorporated into their roads.

The von Koskulls were a charming couple with three nice, little kids. Their house was lovely, large, and comfortable, and all I had to do was speak my mother tongue as clearly as possible and baldfacedly correct the English pronunciation of anybody struggling with it. The families I consorted with were nearly all Finlanders. Finlanders are Finnish citizens of Swedish descent who speak only Swedish among themselves. After a month, I was able to understand Swedish fairly well, and I even could express some simple phrases in that language. One of the very few sentences which remains to me is a useful one: "Tak ska Du har." (Many decades later, Brita -Baroness von Koskull- came to visit us in Milwaukee. We took her to a local base-ball game behind Shorewood High School, and she was absolutely diverted. It was also Brita who insisted, after studying my knitting designs, that I contact the best US handknitting authority (Vogue Knitting) to see if they could use me and my fasci-nation with handknitting.)

I had occasion to visit a Finnish working family, whose low wooden red house consisted of one very large room which served as a living room and kitchen, with a woodburning kitchen stove that kept the whole house warm. Now that I think of it, almost identical to our lovely schoolhouse. The beds were pivoted into recesses in the walls and were let down at bedtime. Winter came with ample snow and fairly cold temperatures, which kept the snowcover intact. It was fun to watch the schoolkids from first grade on, arriving at school on skis. All they had for a binding was a toe strap under which they slid their shoe. Left and right of the schoolhouse door stood a forest of skis, waiting for their owners to come bounding out when the bell rang.

Through this whole period I was deliberately out of touch with Arnold and the events in Germany. Apparently, in Munich, opposite one of the more noble art-museums, there had been constructed two stone memorial buildings: square, with steps going up on all four sides, and columns supporting their square rooves. Hitler had had them placed there, in honor of several of his supporters who had been shot on the spot by some Bavarians who thought that Hitler was intolerable. *Ehrentempel* (temples of honor) was what Hitler called them. Arnold called them *Scheisshaeusl*, being a rather course word for what my dear old father would call Gentlemen's Retiring Rooms. One day, while walking to lunch past these buildings, Arnold was overheard referring to them in the above-mentioned vernacular. I will let him tell the rest in his own words.

After lunch, when we were back in the office, another brewery employee, a member of the Brownshirts, told his co-workers that he had overheard me, and that he would have me "konzentrated" the next day. It was my good luck that an old employee heard this announcement, and went to my uncle, explaining to him the serious-ness of my situation. I was called into my uncle's office and found him with two other directors of the brewery. All three men had serious and concerned faces. My uncle explained the matter to me, and said I was an idiot, but apart from that, what was I going to do now?

I told him I would disappear, and he nodded and wished me luck. Unfortunately, I never saw him again, nor indeed, my father or my brother.

Elizabeth's water color of "The Eck"; Willem Diess's farmhouse.

I never returned to my office, but went directly to the tramway, and to my room in the Kaulbachstrasse. Psychologically, I now felt myself being followed and behind every SA or SS uniform I saw, an informer or a Gestapo official. I quickly made a fire in the coal stove and burned a few banned books: Sinclair Lewis, Thomas Mann etc., put some clothes in my rucksack and took the tram to the Holzkirchen station. There I bought a ticket to Hausham. I sat at a window and the pale, soft grey of the late autumn day slowly melded into the darkening landscape, and by the time we arrived in Holzkirchen, it was dark outside. And dark were the clouds that drew up against our Bavarian land. Many of us felt that very strongly. But what could we do against such a powerful upswelling of crass dictatorship? "Not much, but on the other hand, very little," as the Bavarians say. The whole Nazi philosophy, especially as it had developed by 1936, was foreign to the preponderant majority of Bavarians. Therefore, the already discernable, but not yet exactly detailed disaster was felt and feared increasingly strongly.

I sat in the train and thought of the near future. I had to get out of the country; that was axiomatic for me. I would go to Willem Diess's farm, "The Eck," to take his council. In Hausham, I got off the train and walked through the still Alpine foothills on the little country road, towards the line of hills on which "The Eck" was situated. After climbing the last steep piece of road, I stood before the beautiful, very old farmhouse. Thank god there is a light. I knock; the dog barks and then Elisabeth Diess opens the door. Heartfelt words of greeting. Questions. Relating. Elisabeth the quiet one, the gentle one, is worried. She is alone on the farm. Willem is in the city. She calls him, very adroitly making him acquainted with my position. He asks whether I have my passport. Oh my! I forgot it. Where is it? Instructions. OK. He will be here in two hours with passport and car.

Elisabeth prepared something for me to eat. We sat at the dinner table in the lovely, warm room and talked of the helplessness and powerlessness of all Germans who were non-Nazis and about the tragic fate which all would have to bear - whether Nazi or not. I saw then, with all certainty, the coming of war.

143

Now we hear a motor and a gear-change at the bottom of the hill. It is Willem. He enters the low room with his presence. I am much calmer now. Willem has my passport. During the drive, he has figured everything out sharply and in detail., like the lawyer he is. He says Kiefersfelden is the least dangerous border station. He is going to drop me on a sideroad, about 1 km from the border, and I am to walk with my rucksack to the customs shack and say that I am on a walking tour back into the mountains. My passport is OK; I had been in Salzburg only 14 days previously. However, I am allowed to take only 10 DM across the border.

Elizabeth's return from Finland in January 1937; the freighter following its ice-breaker.

Willem dials the telephone and talks to someone in a strong, highland dialect. After a short conversation, he says to me, "That was Franzl. He is going to meet you at or close to 11:00 pm 1 km on the other side of the border, on the road from Kiefersfelden to Kufstein. He has a black beard, and will have money for you. Now we must go."

Short leave-taking from "The Eck" and Elisabeth. Off we go in the car via Hausham, Miesbach-au-Brannenburg, Oberaudorf. The little towns and villages are asleep, the night sky has clouded over, but the temperature for this time of year is mild. We arrive at a small side road. "This is where I turn around," says Willem. We take a short, intense leave, and embrace.

I walk towards the customs shack, and soon I can see its lights and the pike which hangs across the road. I go straight into the shack. Play it cool! A small round woodstove makes it pleasantly warm for the customs officer, who sits behind the partition. I say, "Heil Hitler".

"Alilla," he replies. "Ja, where do you want to go so late at night?"

"Since the weather stays so nice, I want to go back into the mountains for a few days." I give him my passport. He pulls out a card index and checks under Z. I am sure there is nothing in there . . yet. True. But now he fingers through the telex strips which were recently spit into a wire basket. I begin to sweat. Then it is over. He swings the stamp and slams it like a trump ace onto my passport.

"Good night, Heil Hitler."

"Alilla." I can hardly dare to believe it. I am in Austria - in those days still a free country. I speed up; the road is getting very dark. A small wind wakes up and rustles now and then in the dry leaves. I come to a wooded stretch. All of a sudden there is a rustling which is louder than that of the wind, and my eyes, now used to the dark, discern a stocky man climbing out of the ditch.

"Would you be Zimmermann?"

"Ja, are you the Franzl?"

"Ja, I be him. Here is the 100DM from Willem Diess. And now I wish you good luck. God be with you." We shake hands and he disappears into the woods.

After an hour's walking, I see the lights of Kufstein. My steps reverberate through the empty streets; it is past midnight. My memory leads me on to the Auracher Lochl. Ah, it is still open. I sit down at a small round oaken table and order a liter of Terlaner.

Elizabeth's passport photo. 1937

Of all this, and Arnold's subsequent working his way to Switzerland, I knew nothing. I was experiencing life in the Koskull house, enhanced by the Baron's love for music. He had an extensive library of classical records, and almost every evening we would listen to beautiful concerts. One of his favorite composers, of course, was Jan Sibelius.

For Christmas, I took a boat to Sweden's capital, Stockholm, where I stayed with a family whose daughter had once stayed with my family near Harrow. I'd never - and never shall - experience a similar Christmas. It started at breakfast time on Dec. 24th and lasted well into the beginning of January. Many old traditions and customs surfaced during this enchanted period. At a certain time, Santa Lucia appeared with a wreath on her head

Wedding party on Thames; Marge clowning.

in which burning candles wavered and spread a magic light in the room. "Julbocks" made of straw lurked in the Christmas tree and at midnight on Dec. 31st, we all jumped off chairs into the New Year!

It was Kurt Scharff who met me there in Stockholm and told me of Arnold's plight. I immediately wrote to Arnold and we arranged to meet again in Brussels where he would be overseeing some Belgian malthouses for the Liebman Brewery in America. So, to make a long story short, we decided that it would be a good thing to get married and emigrate to America. Our little wedding was quite touching: in the registry office at Harrow, not far from my family near Harrow-on-the-Hill. Then a wedding-lunch in our house on Draycott Avenue, and a reception party in a barge on the Thames, right after which Arnold and I climbed into the family "caravan" and set off in a Westerly direction towards my beloved Cornwall. We camped on some of

the lovely beaches with their rocky cliffs. I suppose you'd call this a honeymoon, and of course it was. When it was over, we visited various consulates and other offices in London and achieved two passports which enabled us to bid farewell to GB and to set foot in the US. End of another period.

Cornish coast.

145

CHAPTER EIGHT

A MITTFUL OF MITTENS

In the early '40s, we had a house in the quiet countryside of New York State, in Gardnerville. There we lived across the road from another immigrant family, the Peters'. Our two houses were the only ones on this side of the Rutgers Kill. On the other side was the village -- five houses.

Across the meadow between us ran a narrow grassy path made by the children running to each other's houses to play. The Peters' were Norwegian, and Mrs. Peters was always called "Honey", firstly because she called everybody else "Honey", and secondly because she was so sweet.

When the time came for us to move (the frequent fate of newcomers to this country), Honey Peters came across the grassy path with a farewell gift: a pair of beautiful handknitted mittens from her home country. They were accepted with great pleasure, and worn and cherished for many years afterwards.

As their palms wore thin they were darned. And darned. And darned. At last they survived only as relics of those golden summers and snowy winters when all the kids were little. They were worn seldom, and gently.

One day I took a look at them wondering if sewn-on knitted patches would give them a longer lease on life. I considered them again; why not a patch large enough to cover the whole palm? And the thumb? Why not a complete cover for the whole front of each mitten? In bright red? Why not?

They are smallish mittens, about 4" wide and 10.5" long, so I took strong wool, used garter-stitch, and cast on 14 stitches. After 7 ridges I cast on 7 more stitches at one side, so that it jutted out, and worked a further 14 ridges on all 21 stitches. I then decreased

Garter stitch re-palming on an ancient pair of Norwegian Mittens.

one stitch at the beginning of each row until all the stitches were gone. From the 7 cast-on stitches, I knitted up 7, and worked about 10 ridges for the inside of the thumb. A pity to spoil my sequence of sevens, but one musn't be too particular, and this piece had to be long enough to cover the place where the worst holes had occured. The red pieces were stitched neatly to the palm and thumb of each mitten, and Honey's present had a second life ahead of it.

The mittens are warmer than ever before.

Thank you, Honey, and thank you for the memory of those snowbound winters, and golden summers when all the kids fished and swam in the Rutgers Kill.

NORWEGIAN MITTENS

SIZE: Large adult. 4.5" wide at palm, 7.5" from tip to wrist, 11" total length.
MATERIALS: 3oz each of two colors of medium-weight wool; we used Homespun & 2-ply Sheepswool. An 11.5" circular needle, and/or a set of d.p. needles of a size to give you wanted gauge (about #2-4).
GAUGE: 6 stitches to 1".

For a cute border, you may use **I-Cord "casting on"** *(see chapter 4)* in a third color:

Knit 56 rowlets of I-Cord, weave the ends, and knit up 56 stitches from the resulting ring of I-Cord. Purl the first round. Knit one round. Work a **Cuff Pattern,** maybe this one:

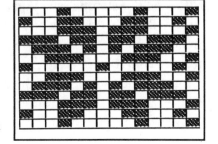

Cuff Pattern

147

Knit 1 round, Purl 1 round.
For a bit of wrist demarcation: knit 2 together 13 times at wrist front. Knit 6-8 rounds. Purl 1 round.

Now the fun begins:
Mark 25 stitches for the **main pattern** across the back.
Isolate 3 stitches at either side of main pattern for the **stripes** that will run up the side of the mitten. Of the 13 decreased stitches, increase just 5 of them, evenly spaced across the palm.
The remaining 8 stitches will be gradually increased in the **thumb gusset** as follows: mark 3 stitches for the start of the thumb (the first 3 stitches following the side stripe; left or right hand). After 3 rounds, increase 1 stitch each side of the 3 marked stitches. After 3 more rounds, increase 1 stitch each side of the 5 marked stitches, then each side of 7, then of 9. Thus 8 stitches are increased for the thumb, which now consists of 11 stitches. I like to keep the thumb in stripes of alternate colors.

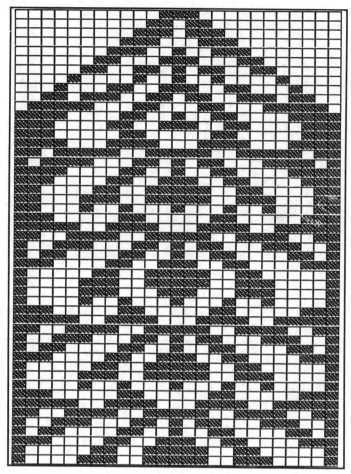

This is not an authentic Norwegian pattern, but one of my own which I call "Winter Spruce". Note how the Knitter's Graph Paper (at a 5:7 ratio) used for this chart doesn't match the finished knitting? Working firmly with thickish wool, in color-pattern has taught me a surprising fact: the row and stitch gauges to one inch are nearly the same! The mittens on the opposite page ended up at 6 stitches and 6.5 rows to 1 inch.

At wanted height for thumb-opening (try the partial mitten on to determine this), perform the
THUMB TRICK: With a contrasting color, knit the 11 thumb stitches. Put them back on the left needle, and re-knit them in the regular pattern colors, as if nothing had happened. When the mitten is done, remove the contrasting color, and pick up the revealed stitches onto 3 d.p. needles; there will

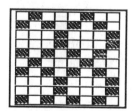

Palm pattern

148

*Palms showing Thumb Trick
and striped thumb.*

Finished Norwegian mittens

be about 22 of them. PLUS, pick up the running thread at each corner, and twist it into a stitch to prevent holes. On the upper edge, stitches will be less obvious.

Work the thumb to wanted length, and decrease at the tip by either: K2 tog around, K 1 round, K2 tog around...*or*, establish side points, and double decrease there every round if you want the top of the thumb to match the top of the hand.

TIP: Working around on 4 d.p. needles on very few stitches can be a slippery business. Using <u>wooden</u> needles will help.

Here is an alternate Main Pattern: a very typical Norwegian snowflake design.

149

SIDEWAYS MYSTERY MITTENS ON TWO NEEDLES IN GARTER-STITCH

How's this for a new approach to knitting mittens?

SIZE: Average adult. (Change the size by varying the weight of wool, and size of needle you use.)

GAUGE: 5 stitches to 1".

MATERIALS: 1 4oz skein 2-ply Sheepswool, Fisherman Wool, Homespun or 2-ply Icelandic Wool. A circular needle (or a pair of needles) of a size to give you the above gauge.

An in-progress, and a finished Mystery Mitten

CAST ON 59 stitches. You will be knitting back and forth in garter-stitch; down the inside of the thumb and up the outside of the index finger.

ROW 1 (wrong side): K11 for thumb, P1, K1, P1, K15 for forefinger, P1 (center stitch), then reverse matters: K15, P1, K1, P1, K11. Those purled stitches are always purled on the wrong side, which makes a knit chain on the right side; an elegant line, and a guide for the shaping. It is a good idea to grab a handful of coilless safety pins, and put a marker in each of the purl stitches until the pattern gets established.

On odd-numbered rows, KNIT the K stitches and PURL the P stitches.

On Even-numbered rows, all stitches are K, and the M(ake) 1 increases occur.

ROW 2: K12, M1, K1, M1, K1, M1, K15, M1, K1, M1, K15, M1, K1, M1, K1, M1, K12.

ROW 4: K12, M1, K3, M1, K1, M1, K17, M1, K1, M1, K17, M1, K1, M1, K3, M1, K12.

ROW 6: K12, M1, K5, M1, K1, M1, K19, M1, K1, M1, K19, M1, K1, M1, K5, M1, K12.

Continue thus, making a stitch on the inside of the first and last chained stitch, and on either side of the other three chains.

When there are a total of 5 ridges (10 rows), STOP the center increase.

When there are 8 ridges, leave 11 stitches at either end on pieces of wool (thumb), and cut out the two outer increases.

Now start to decrease one stitch at the end of each row.

I like to *work to within 2 stitches of the

150

end, wool forward, slip 2 as if to purl. Turn, K2 tog through back loops. Repeat from *

Continue with the 2 remaining increases. When there are 10 ridges, start decreasing at the center as follows: work to within 1 stitch of the center, Slip 2 together knit-wise, K1, Pass 2 slipped stitches over. A double decrease.

When there are 15 ridges, knit to the center, make one last double decrease, and weave the sides *(see garter-stitch weaving in appendix)* until 30 wrist stitches remain.

WRIST: Work back and forth on the 30 stitches for 6 ridges.

CUFF: Increase by working K2, M1 across (45 stitches). Work straight for as long as you like for the cuff. Cast off in purl on the right side, leaving a generous tail.

Sew side seam. WEAVE thumb and sew thumb tip together. Or, if you are fussy, pick up top selvedge stitches from the thumb, work 1 or 2 rows of K1, K2 tog. Then sew up.

The Left and Right hands are the same. Give them in threes!

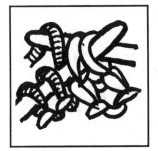

To Decrease at end of row: Work to within 2 sts of end. Wool forward. Slip 2 p'wise. Turn. K2 tog at beginning of next row.

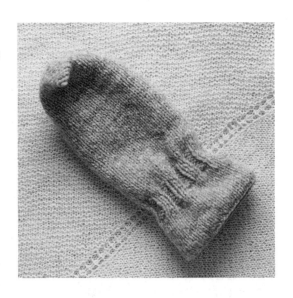

Double-thick Jogger's Mittens

CURLED-TIP JOGGER'S MITTENS (WITH OR WITHOUT *AFTERTHOUGHT THUMBS*)

Wisconsin winters can be bitter, and our jogger's mutter about cold hands and freezing thumbs. You say, slip your thumb out of its mitten thumb and warm it up with your fingers. They say no; they don't want to... couldn't mittens be made without thumbs? Clever joggers. Mittens may indeed be made without thumbs, you say - secretly rejoicing that you'll not have to bother with them for once.

As you work your way up the first thumbless mitten, ideas come crowding: let's nip in the wrist a bit to foil the icy blasts that want to blow in at the cuff. Why not a bit of ribbing on fewer stitches?

Now up the hand you go, and another idea surfaces: remember that old

151

curled-tip mitten you came up with in 1960-something? And, wouldn't a double-mitten be twice as warm? Remember the Very Warm Hat?

Let us incorporate all these ideas into one mitten. And, if and when the jogger becomes a civilian again, an After-thought Thumb is a simple and painless operation.

JOGGER'S THUMBLESS MITTEN

SIZE: Average adult hand.
GAUGE: 5 stitches to 1".
MATERIALS: 1 4oz skein 2-ply Sheepswool, Homespun, Fisherman or 2-ply Icelandic Wool. An 11.5" circular needle, and/or a set of d.p. needles.

CAST ON 48 stitches. For a Doubled Mitten, do not worry about a border, but just begin knitting around.
After 2-3" (wanted cuff length), decrease sharply by working K2, K2 together around.
WRIST: Switch to K2, P2 ribbing for a good inch (about 9-10 rounds).
Increase back up to 48 by working K3, M1 around.
Continue straight for 5 - 5.5", or until you reach the top of the little finger.
CURLED TIP: Mark 1 stitch at the center back. Knit to within one stitch of it, and work a Double Decrease as follows:
Sl 2, K1, P2SSO (Slip 2 together knitwise, Knit 1, pass the 2 slipped stitches over.)

TIP: It is sometimes difficult for new knitters to keep a series of these beautiful

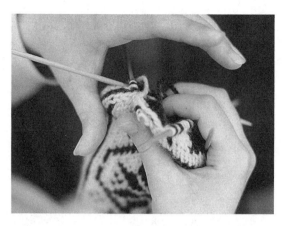

If you are new to d.p. needles, try this: arrange the three needles so that needle #1 (the needle you are about to knit into) rests over #2. Take the needles in your left hand so that the cross formed by #1 and #2 rests in the crotch of your left thumb.

The middle finger of your left hand will control #2, and off you knit. Again, we recommend wooden needles to new knitters, as you will not have to worry about the needles sliding out of the stitches

decreases in a straight line. Think of it as turning 3 stitches into 1, and the middle of the 3 stitches is the 'marked' stitch. So, the stitch you dig into when you 'slip 2 tog' is the stitch that will consume its neighbors. And it will be the center of the next group of 3 that you will turn into 1.

Repeat this decrease every *other* round two times, then *every* round until just under half the stitches remain (about 20).

Fold them side to side, and weave them together. *(See stocking-stitch weaving in appendix)*

Slip your hand into the finished mitten. Doesn't the Curled Tip conform beautifully to your fingers? Doesn't it feel like an ancient mitten that has molded itself to your hand after years of wear?

Once you see the mitten with a hand in it, you, like I, may be unable to resist running to your local fabric-and-notions store to buy a packet of those swivelling eyes people use for stuffed animals. Sew them on, and each mitten will acquire character and individuality. And there the thumb will be, snugged in with the fingers, helping with the show.

INNER MITTEN:

From the right side, knit up one stitch for each cast on stitch around the lower edge.

If you want the mittens to be reversible, work the inner mitten on the same number of stitches as the outer.

If you want the inner mitten to serve as a lining only, then reduce its size slightly by decreasing 4 stitches after knitting the first round.

Proceed as for first mitten.

153

IF THUMBLESSNESS CEASES TO CHARM

AFTERTHOUGHT THUMB: Try the mitten on, and feel around for your thumb-knuckle. Snip one stitch (one side of a stitch, actually) and unravel about 3 or 4 stitches in each direction, which will reveal about 15 stitches top and bottom. Pick them up on 3 d.p. needles (wooden needles are good to prevent slipping and sliding).

Begin at the palm end, and leave a longish tail of wool to neaten and strengthen this sensitive spot later on.

Knit around for about 15-20 tiny rounds. K 2 together around. Break the wool and thread it through the remaining stitches. Fasten securely (maybe skimming the wool down the inside of the thumb to the outer corner, and neatening it).

This Afterthought Thumb business allows you the leeway to place the thumb on the palm, or sticking out from the side of the mitten; knitter's choice.

Afterthought Thumb. Snip into a stitch.

THE MITRED MITTEN:

Once you have mastered 4 needles, try working on 5. It is usually more practical to divide a circular bit of knitting into quarters than into thirds.

SIZE: average adult.

GAUGE: 5 stitches to 1"

MATERIALS: 1 4oz skein 2-ply Sheepswool, Homespun, Fisherman, or 2-ply Icelandic Wool.

Using I-Cord "Cast On", knit 48 rowlets of I-Cord, weave end to beginning, Pick up 48 stitches from the cord, and put 12 stitches on each of 4 needles.

Join and purl one round.

ESTABLISH MITRE:

*1st needle: SSK, K to last stitch, M1, K1.

2nd needle: K1, M1, K to last 2 stitches, K2 together.

3rd needle: repeat first needle.

4th needle: repeat second needle.

First round done.

2nd ROUND: K12 on all 4 needles.

Repeat from * for 8", or until 1/2" shy of little finger tip. (Ignore the thumb for now.)

STOP INCREASING, but

CONTINUE DECREASING

and the point will appear.

When 8 stitches remain, weave them together, or run the wool through and finish them off.

AFTERTHOUGHT THUMB:

The finished mitten should be about 11" long from cuff to tip. Try it on.

At 5.5" (or where you can feel the joint of the thumb), draw a deep breath and snip into one stitch.

Unravel in both directions as described in

Mitred Mittens with I-Cord ties.

the Jogger's Mitten - but this time the thumb opening will go on the bias. Pick up the liberated stitches, and knit the thumb, as before.

I-CORD WRIST TIES:

Since we did not shape for the wrist during the knitting, you can knit about 12-14" of Free-Standing I-Cord, and just thread it through the back of the finished mitten ... about 3 inches apart (1.5" each side of center-back). When tied, this will nip in the wrist nicely.

154

. . .Digressions

We landed in the US in the Fall of 1937 - my God how long ago - after a stormy voyage in the good ship S. S. American Banker out of Tilbury Docks in London. It took ten days, most of which I spent below in the throes of sea-cum-morning sickness. I did have one meal in the dining-room, fricasseed chicken on rice, which I always love, and wedges of incredible American iceberg lettuce, of which I had never seen anything so wonderful and crisp. Then I retired to the bowels of the ship, and lived off orange juice, which I never really believed flowed like water in the US, but which I now tended to believe did. I stumbled up on deck to view the Statue of Liberty one cold and blowy day, and all of a sudden, there we were going through customs.

We were met by Perry Lion, the latter being the very friend of Arnold's who had been the recipient of my thank-you note at the bank in Munich. Perry had several years of immigrant experience behind him, and swept us off in his second-hand Buick roadster (later ours - an enormous boat of a car) to a furnished room in Jackson Heights which he had most kindly reserved for us. The first thing we did that day was to go to Manhattan and get our Declaration of Intention, as the first step to becoming American citizens. As I say, this was 1937 and prospects in the US were bleak indeed. No jobs. In those days, in order to enter the country, one had to put one's hand on one's breakfast and swear to almightygod that one didn't even have a whisper of a job prospect. Unemployment was rife, and immigrants were looked upon sideways, as being intent on cutting out the honest American workman, as lord knows they were, or why would they have taken the trouble to come all that way?

Elizabeth and baby Thomas. 1939

So there we were, pregnant, jobless, and in debt. We had borrowed a slug of money from Uncle Benny in order to prove to the immigration chaps that we had means and were not desperate vagrants. We had landed in a country which I had had the temerity, up until then, to hate and fear. Those terms are of course overstrong, but the tendancy of the American in Europe to exaggerate to the European things which are already incredible, does not enhance the desirability of his country. Then he drinks too hard, and shows off, and drools over European antiquities, until one thinks my God, what unspeakable barbarities has he left behind? Of course, you only notice the loud ones. This view was sturdily encouraged by the movies, of course, and you can only imagine the expectations of the foreigner coming to the US. If we could only, then and before, have had a prophetic vision of the friendly midwest and our dear Schoolhouse, we would have saved our pennies for the trip from our tenderest years, and I would have greeted the Statue of Liberty with a glad cry, instead of rather apprehensive gloom on that bleak October day.

After our first move towards citizenship, Arnold telephoned Mr. Schuelein, whom he had known in Munich, and who represented the greatest hope of securing a job. The hope turned out to be justified, and within less than a week, he started at Liebman's brewery in Brooklyn at the unheard-of salary of 25 bucks a week. I was mostly alone in our room for those first few weeks, eating out of cans (an anticipated wonder, but more expensive than I had imagined, and canned lemon juice - a great disappointment) interspersed with baked beans at Bickfords. Every day I made long excursions in the neighborhood looking for furnished apartments, but being thoroughly at sea in a foreign environment, I looked in the wrong places like Bushwick Ave, and Forest Hills.One Sunday, Perry kindly took us househunting.

A place in Richmond Hill turned out to be too expensive, but the woman told us she thought there was an empty apartment up the road, so we went there and it was. The Leiths owned a 3-story frame house half a block from *Jamaica-r-avenoo*, and the attic floor was for rent. We could hardly believe our eyes. For $35 a month, a tiny tolerably-furnished living-room, with just room for a bed and dresser in the bedroom, and three closets - clothes-closet, bathroom and kitchen respectively. Mrs. Leith was red-headed, 40, childless, and very nice, and would babble of somebody she called the Earl of Boyner in the basement. When we moved in the next week and stowed our books and big trunk in the basement, we found him to be the oil burner. So we settled in. I paid a visit to Dr. Retzbach, a good old German doctor, and settled down to saving money and being pregnant; Tom was due the following June.

Our main energies were directed to saving up enough to pay back Uncle Benny. I started a savings acount at the Richmond Hill Savings Bank, and trotted in there every payday with my little book. We of course lived on the least we could, and I budgeted $14 weekly, I believe, for food, or was it $7. It seems incredible - I've still got that little book somewhere. We lived largely off delicatessen from Gesau and Kamp, and Campbell's Soup, which I was very expert at heating up. I had wonderful times in the Greengrocer's - Jahn's - because I simply couldn't comprehend being able to buy green vegetables all through the winter. Our consumption of greenbeans was quite staggering, and as for mushrooms - I think they were all of 20 cents a pound, and I would buy them by the quarter pound and cook them up in some kind of bacon gravy - still one of my favorite dishes. For Christmas we splurged: chicken fricassee, and a boughten *stollen* for 25 cents.

Arnold and baby Thomas. 1939

The Chevy parked on 113th Street.

Arnold worked on some kind of night shift which necessitated his getting up at 2:30 every morning and being home again by noon. So we regulated our lives accordingly. What I chiefly remember of that spring of 1938 is lying on our stomachs on the bed which we pulled up beneath the window, and watching the traffic and the High School kids on 113th St. The street was tree-lined, and outside our house a large tree unfolded its leaves into quite unexpected gorgeousness. It was a common-or-garden swamp maple, but we did not know this, and called it our *Zierbaum.* After Tom was born we continued this twisted-around schedule, and it proved most practical. I got all the wash and chores done before it was light in the morning, then fussed with Tom until Arnold came home at noon. After lunch, we went mostly to Forest Park, and then all to bed at 6 pm. We were quite astonished at the weather: the heat, and the tropic-like sudden rainstorms surprise me to this day. Also thunder storms in the winter, and especially the long stretches of wonderfully clear days. I remember hanging out my washing day after day, and saying to Mrs. Hutchinson next door "What a WONDERFUL day" in a very limey accent, and she being as surprised at my astonishment as I was at the weather. Of *course* it was a beautiful day - what else?

What else? A thousand little niggling memories occur to me, but how can I convey the special atmosphere of any given time. The bran-new baby in the bran-new buggy. The visits to the movie on the same block while the Leiths watched the baby. There we were, quite alone, unless you count the ubiquitous Perry. When I returned from the hospital with this terrifying infant, no one so much as brought up a piece of pie or a bowl of soup. We didn't think it odd, but with my later knowledge of the US, I certainly do now. New York is a suspicious city. I suppose it comes from having to act as strainer to the dregs of Europe. So many people pass through - after all, we did too, in time - and some of the most undesirable ones become stuck there. Neither was there anything more than spiritual support coming out of Europe, to which we had by now repaid the money borrowed. The Zimmermanns did send a trunk of used babyclothes and an old suit from Arnold's brother, Heiner. The Lloyd-Joneses sent many dear little sweaters plus, from Mummy, enough money to buy a pram.

Arnold and Thomas (in his knitted bathing suit) at the beach.

157

After a time, Arnold was earning a little more at the brewery, though his position was still only a sort of glorified bottlewasher in the lab. Our savings were mounting up, and the first thing we treated ourselves to was a little old yellow Chevy for $30. With this, after the second Christmas, we started househunting, as the little upstairs apartment was starting to give at the seams. By scanning the papers, we ended up at Krues's house, which intrigued us the moment we saw it; a little thin old duplex at the back of a large garden, left over from farming days. We had the left, or South end, which had its own front door, a large sunny kitchen and a sliver of a living-room downstairs, and upstairs a large bedroom and an equal sliver plus a bathroom with a tub and a john but no basin. No heat. Hot water by means of a gas-heater. Rent, $27 a month. So in we moved, buying a bed bran-new from Gimbels for that purpose. There we were in our little old duplex at 8624 124th St. We stayed there for almost exactly three years, during which time Lloie was born and then Meg in 1942.

We painted over the fireplace in *Bayerische Rautenmuster*, put up pretty blue

The tree-bench around the pear tree, and Thomas in the rocker. 124th Street, Richmond Hill.

percale curtains (later red corduroy), and, a great triumph of carpentry, shelves between the two east windows. These were used to display the pale blue open stock china which we commissioned from the F. W. Woolworth Company, and under them was the "Shadbolt Table". The latter was made for us by a neighbor for $12 and remains with us to this day. Then it was covered with a piece of oilcloth representing a map of Europe. The table at the wall end took to accumulating letters, useful magazines, etc, and I don't think it ever got quite clear. The sink at least was cleared once a day, because the drainboard was over the washtub, and that is where the master Tom took his daily bath, and where I washed the clothes - no machine. The water pipes ran along the floor under the windows, and we thought it would be a nice idea to box them in. It was a great labor and looked fine. It insulated them nicely too, and one cold winter - the Pearl Harbor winter as a matter of fact, when the kids and I were up in Gardnerville - the whole works froze. It was hellish cold in winter, but of course we didn't notice this. The rooms were ineffably light and sunny, the garden was a delight, and right outside the front door was a big, ancient pear tree, which used to bloom right into the bathroom window, and produced wonderful fruit. Around this Arnold built a tree-bench which was greatly admired by one and all. And there we were. I'm sure

158

everyone thought we were nuts, but we were together, and healthy and saving money, and what more can an immigrant family want?

By now we longed for the countryside, and having heard rumors of the beauty of New York State, we set out over the George Washington Bridge one day in 1941, looking for our own place for weekends. The Middletown real estate man, Mr. Adams, took us around to some less favorable locations, and then drove deeper and deeper into the true countryside. We stopped on a bridge over a charming little river and spied the house with a For Sale sign. "Well, that's a nice house," we thought. "They're asking $1,500," he said, "but I think you can get it for $1,200." He was right. Within a week

The house at Gardnerville. 1941.

we traveled up to Orange County again, and bought it, along with its two and a half acres, which sloped down over the country road to the river, called the Rutgers Kill. It had kitchen and living room downstairs, and upstairs two and a half bedrooms. And an out-house. No running water, but a splendid well-with-a-bucket-on-a-rope outside the kitchen door. From the house you could see the river, the bridge, and surrounding shallow hills, and about 6 neighbors' houses, which together with the crossroads was the totality of Gardnerville.

Elizabeth painting in the meadow. Gardnerville, NY.

The house was what is now called a "handyman's special" and needed extensive work. This was done by Arnold and a salty old neighbor up the hill, Russell Stewart. Now we found out what neighbors in America really were. "We'll fetch her" Russell used to say when confronted by some insoluble problem of carpentry or plumbing or just plain wit, and fetch her they always did. He could do anything that fixing up a house called for, and had a real joy in tackling things. The day we ripped out the old kitchen ceiling, it was he who swung the first wrecking-bar at the thing, and I can see his face now, shining with joy amid the dust,

159

Elizabeth and Meg. Gardnerville, 1945.

plaster and mouse nests which showered down on him. My chief friend was Sara Laine who lived up the valley with her family of eight boys. She was a real treasure, and helped me aquaint myself with many of the neighbors, the village, and the nearby towns of Middletown, Johnstown, and Slate Hill. We missed nary a weekend let alone summer vacations at Gardnerville until we uprooted ourselves and moved to New Hope, PA. However, Gardnerville remains in our hearts and memories to this day.

By 1946, Arnold had become assistant Brewmaster at Liebman's Rheinegold Brewery in Brooklyn. Then he received an offer to be Brewmaster at a smaller (and very cosy) one in Trenton, NJ called Trenton Old Stock, which he accepted. He went on ahead into a rented room, and we started preparing for a move. One day, listening with half an ear to the radio, I somehow heard of people wanting to sell their house in Northern New Jersey. "Come on kids" and I packed all three into the second car (yes, we'd become fair copies of Americans) and off we set. By noon we'd found the house, but discovered it was all a mistake, being the result of a casual comment to a friend who had spread the "news" far and wide, to end up on the morning-radio.

"But go south of here," they said. "The countryside is very nice and you can cross the Delaware river at Lambertville." So we did, crossing the river to New Hope. What a suitably named town. In it we found a 90-year-old river house,with the actual Delaware River at the bottom of the garden, and the barge canal across the street in the front. The house had fascinating floorboards perhaps 12 - 15 inches wide, and shiny. So we made our move and stayed there for almost four years; in fact, it's still in the family. There were very good schools for the three (now fast

160 S. Main Street, New Hope, Pa. 1946

160

Elizabeth in the back yard of the New Hope house,
with the Delaware River behind her. 1949.

growing) kids, and a strongly art-oriented population. It was only a few miles up the river from Trenton and everything was going smoothly until, alas, Trenton Old Stock folded in 1949. For three nervous months Arnold was unemployed, but the news soon penetrated to Wisconsin, the capitol of the brewing industry and home of the Jos. Schlitz Brewing Company, and he had a new job. Splendid. Arnold, again, went on ahead and when things were settled, I left the house sadly (to be rented), and set off - with cats, kids and goldfish - for Milwaukee.

And what about knitting? Well, I knew from my English upbringing that the moment Tom was born, he should be well-supplied with knitted woollen garments, and I started off with several small jackets and sweaters, gradually leading up to a pair of longies, at that point not at all frequently observed in the US. Thomas's Tomten jacket was also ahead of its time in this country; a reminiscence of something I'd observed in Scandinavia. This was an instant heirloom for the three kids, (see p. 124), and is surely tucked away somewhere right now. There are now two grandchildren (Chris and Meg's Cully and Liesl) who are enjoying their own era of woollens, mostly knitted by "Oma". Is knitting wonderful, or isn't it?

161

Meg and Liesl in the Aran coats.

CHAPTER NINE

AN ARAN COAT

It has been over thirty years since I knitted my first Aran sweater on commission from *Vogue Pattern* magazine. At that time I had never seen or heard of Aran sweaters, and I blindly followed the instructions with which Vogue had presented me. There were no drawings or photographs to show me what I was knitting, so you can imagine what a surprise and delight it was to observe the unfamiliar, yet fascinating travelling stitches and cables which emerged from my needles. That was in 1956, and I believe, when the garment was published in 1957, it was the first Aran sweater ever presented in the U.S. *Vogue* had apparently found the pattern through their British branch.

After having completed two versions of the sweater worked back and forth on straight needles (using lovely oiled Sheepswool, of course), I realized how much easier and more sensible it would be to knit these intriguing designs on *circular* needles, with the front of the work always facing the knitter, eliminating the necessity of (when working back on the wrong side) peering over the top of the needles to see where you were.

After several more Arans (worked in the round by now), my obsession shifted from copying the patterns from Gladys Thompson's splendid book, PATTERNS FOR GUERNSEYS, JERSEYS & ARANS, to experi-

Elizabeth in her Aran coat.

163

menting with new designs of my own. (By the way, I corresponded with Gladys Thompson when her book was first published in the U.K., and learned from her that the Aran chapter at the end of the book had been stuck on as an afterthought. Also, she had written the Guernsey and Jersey instructions in the round, as the original garments had been knitted. But the publisher caused her to change them all to back and forth pieces on straight needles, because that was how British knitters preferred to work! Ah, history!) My experimentation led to several new patterns, among them the Sheepfold design shown in this coat. I was pleased enough with Sheepfold to send it to Barbara Walker. She had included a request for un-known knitting patterns at the end of her new book, *A TREASURY OF KNITTING PATTERNS,* and I thought it would be foolish to pass up such an opportunity. Barbara kindly included Sheepfold in the *SECOND TREASURY*, and our subsequent correspondence resulted in Barbara steering me to her publisher at Scribner's, which led to the publishing of my first book, *KNITTING WITHOUT TEARS* in 1971.

Meanwhile, we had commissioned our woollen mill to custom-spin a very thick, natural, unbleached wool of four un-spun plies, which we called Sheepsdown. I was struck by the possibility of an Aran coat; elegant, warm, and as far as I knew, as yet unknitted. As testimony to the beauty and strength of Sheepsdown, the original coat is now well over 20 years old, has been worn fairly steadily by Lloie, Meg and me, and is still hanging in there. It is rather thin now, but I wore it happily and warmly all last winter which prompted us to include it here.

CIRCULAR, HOODED ARAN COAT

Exposition

The original Aran Coat was made as follows: I knitted up some Sheepsdown on a 16" #10.5 needle to see what gauge I would get working over cables and travelling stitches. With my gauge determined, I cast sufficient body stitches onto a 24" needle and knitted around, keeping a few neutral stitches at the center front for cutting later on.

I thought of the whole body as consisting of quarters; the left-front Sheepfold mirrored the right-front, and they were repeated on the back. Up the body I sailed, thoroughly enjoying myself, so fast was my progress with such thick wool and needles. At about 20-22", I set this huge chunk of knitting aside, and started the sleeves on about 25% of the body stitches. I increased gently (two stitches every four rounds) until I had nearly half the number of body stitches. From then on, I continued straight to wanted length to underarm.

Meg wearing the original coat; Liesl in the new copy.

The body and sleeves were united onto the 24" needle, leaving underarm stitches of both body and sleeves on pieces of wool, and on up the yoke I knitted. After a few inches I began a single-decrease at each of four points where the sleeves and body met (causing the body to eat up the sleeve stitches), and finished off with epaulets, working back and forth nibbling up stitches horizontally, until what remained looked about right for a neck opening.

For the hood, I gathered up the neck stitches onto the 16" needle, and started increasing right away: two stitches at center-back every second round, until the hood looked as if it would fit a head. Then straight on up to the top, unshaped. Finally, I cut down the front of both hood and body, wove hood-top and underarms, added wide garter-stitch front borders, twisted up toggle ties, sewed on toggles, added Afterthought Pockets ... and voilá! *Ein stück Kuchen!*

On the following pages, we offer you more-or-less detailed instructions for this coat. We suggest the Dropped Shoulder version for Unsure or New Knitters, as it is easier to knit the coat in three pieces rather than have the body and sleeves all on the needle at once.

The circle schematic on the next page is Meg's method of planning an Aran garment, and a good one it is. You may easily substitute in any patterns you like, as well as insert or delete patterns to adjust the circumference of *your* coat.

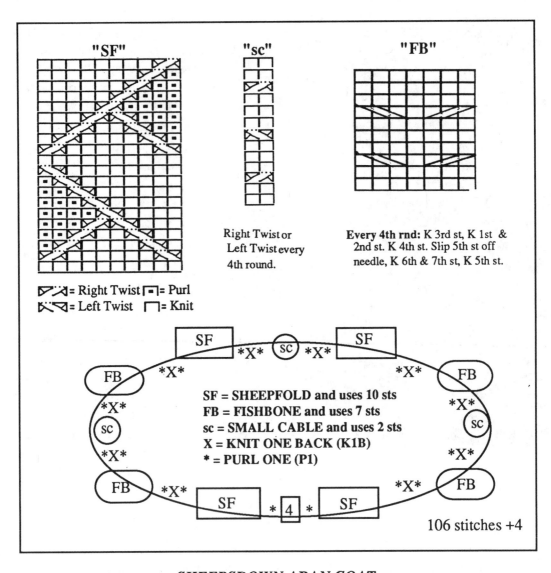

"SF"

"sc"

Right Twist or
Left Twist every
4th round.

"FB"

Every 4th rnd: K 3rd st, K 1st &
2nd st. K 4th st. Slip 5th st off
needle, K 6th & 7th st, K 5th st.

▷◁ = Right Twist ▯ = Purl
◁▷ = Left Twist ▯ = Knit

SF = SHEEPFOLD and uses 10 sts
FB = FISHBONE and uses 7 sts
sc = SMALL CABLE and uses 2 sts
X = KNIT ONE BACK (K1B)
* = PURL ONE (P1)

106 stitches +4

SHEEPSDOWN ARAN COAT

SIZE: 42" around body. Approximately 34" length from shoulder to lower edge.
GAUGE: 2.5 stitches to one inch.
MATERIALS: 14 4oz skeins of Sheepsdown (allowing for hood), or some other thick, soft, wool. A 16" and 24" circular needle of a size to give you wanted gauge (we used #10.5). 5 wooden toggle buttons.

OPTIONAL: 11.5" circular needle in a smaller size for the Snow Cuff and pocket linings, which will need a 4oz skein of 3-ply Sheepswool in a matching shade ... or contrasting. How about Scarlet?
SO: Multiply your gauge times wanted circumference (2.5 x 42"), and with the 24" needle, **CAST ON** the resulting Key Number [K] (106 stitches).

ADD an extra 4 stitches, and keep them in stocking-stitch at the center front for machine stitching and cutting later on.

Establish the patterns according to the schematic on the opposite page, and work around to wanted length:

*to **underarm** for the Epaulet Version*
*to **shoulder-top** for the Drop-shoulder version.*

(If you are making the Drop-Shoulder version, for ease in cutting the armhole later on, change the "sc"s at the side of the body to plain knit at estimated armhole depth.) Whichever version you are making, you can now put the body aside, and begin the sleeves.

The Snow Cuff is knitted in one with Coat Cuff. Increased sleeve stitches are incorporated into stripes of P2, K1b.

SNOW CUFF (Optional): Using the smaller-sized 11.5" circular needle, and 3-ply Sheepswool, CAST ON 32 stitches. K2, P2 for 4". Increase to 40 stitches and work in plain stocking stitch for 3". Put this aside, and begin the

COAT CUFF: With 16" needle, and Sheepsdown, CAST ON 30 stitches. Establish the patterns as follows:

P2, "SF", P1, "sc", P1, "SF", P2, "sc". The final "sc" is the underarm seamline. Work an increase each side of the seamline every 4th round.

When you have 34 stitches, INSERT the Snow Cuff inside the Coat Cuff with the right side of the Snow Cuff facing the wrong side of the Coat Cuff.

With the two needles parallel, knit the cuffs together, maintaining the Aran pattern sequence.

Because of the gauge difference between the two wools on the two cuffs, you will have to K2 together on the Snow Cuff 6 times to get the 40 stitches to match the 34 stitches of the coat cuff.

Now, abandon the smaller needle, and continue around on the sleeve, gradually incorporating the increased underarm stitches into stripes of P2, K1b, as shown here in the photo.

DROP-SHOULDER VERSION:

Continue increasing to 56-60 stitches. Work straight to wanted length (see Norwegian Pullover chapter to determine sleeve length on this type of garment).

Measure, baste, machine-stitch, and cut as for the Norwegian Pullover in Chapter Seven.

For the hood, front cutting, border, pockets, and toggle ties, see ahead.

EPAULET SHOULDER VERSION:

Increase the sleeves to 50 stitches, and work straight to wanted length to underarm.

Put 14 stitches of sleeves and body on pieces of wool at the underarms, centered directly above the "sc". This is a bit more that the usual 8% of [K], but we are balancing one-half of each "FB" pattern to run up the sides of the sleeve "seams". *(see photo opposite)*

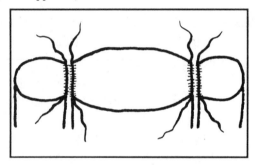

UNITE the sleeves and body onto one needle *(see drawing above)*, as you did on the Seamless Yoke Sweater.

What follows now is not particularly tricky, but is a bit unwieldy, and we recommend a Knitting Buddy to help with the cumbersome part. To knit around in tandom, proceed as follows:

With a second ball of wool, knit half the stitches onto another 24" needle. Sit knee-to-knee with your Knitting Buddy, each of you holding one end of one needle, and one end of the other needle. Put a brightly colored marker at the beginning of the round, and off you go.

One of you will be starting a new round, the other will be finishing the old round. You will each knit a *complete round*, but you will each be knitting only *every other round*.

Knit the stitches as they present themselves, skipping one round when you come to the beginning marker.

It will help enormously if you each knit at the same speed and tension.

So, knit around in pattern, the two of you, for about 2 inches,. You may then want to turn the project over to just one knitting brain for the shoulder shaping.

Elizabeth and Meg knitting around together on the body and sleeves of the coat.
Four-Handed Knitting. (See also page 131)

*The Epaulet shoulder, with half of the Fishbone pattern
running up each side of the sleeve "seam".*

Mark the four raglan points (where the sleeves join the body), and work a *single decrease* at these four points *every* round. You want the body to consume the sleeve stitches, so:

*Beginning at center-front, K to 1st marker, SSK. Knit across sleeve to within one stitch of the 2nd marker, K2 together. Knit across back to 3rd marker, SSK. Knit across sleeve to within one stitch of the 4th marker, K2 together.

Repeat from *, getting rid of 4 stitches every round, until there are only 4 stitches between the markers: the "sc" with a P1 each side of it.

Now, a decision: **IF, for reasons of gauge, or size of the recipient, your yoke is still not deep enough, you can work a bit of a Saddle Shoulder at this point by** *reversing* **the direction of the decreases for 2-3 rounds. Where you were SSK-ing, work K2 together. Where you were Knitting 2 together, work SSK.**

This not only deepens the yoke, but it will "set-in" the shoulders a bit, which will round them nicely. The square shoulders above do not include this bit of shaping, and we rather wish they did.

ACTUAL EPAULET: The knitting is now going to turn a right-angle, as you begin to work back and forth on the 4 remaining stitches, uniting the epaulet to

Back-of-neck-shaping. Note how the Sheepfold goes from 10 to 8 stitches wide, and how an extra half Sheepfold has been snuck onto the back only.

It looks as if we have too many stitches around the neck for the hood, so we want to reduce this number.

Why not reduce the width of each of the 4 Sheepfolds from 10 stitches wide to 8 stitches? Why not? With 8 fewer stitches, the hood circumference seems just right.

OK. So, as we work back and forth (in pattern) across the back from Epaulet to Epaulet, we will K2 tog (or SSK) at *each side* of *each Sheepfold,* one time only, AND at the same time, decrease the Epaulets themselves down to one stitch by working a decrease at the end of each short row. *(See photo below)*

the front and back of the body:

*Work 3, SSK. Turn, work 3, P2 tog. Turn. Repeat from *.

OPTION: This is where Meg , in the video, knitted-back-backwards to prevent having to turn the huge thing in her lap each time.

Continue until you have eaten up 8 stitches alternately on each front and back (16 rows). Work across the back, and repeat the above for the other Epaulet.

RAISING THE NECK-BACK:
This is a bit sticky to explain, but try to stay with us.

We want to raise the back of the neck, and we are also anticipating the hood.

UNITE all remaining stitches around the neck opening for the hood

Close up of the right shoulder Epaulet, decreased down to one stitch when it gets to the neck.

170

(about 48-50, *plus* the center 4 cutting stitches). Decrease the front SF from 10 stitches to 8 in the first hood round.

You will have 2 "SF" running up each side of the hood, with the "sc" at the center back. Because you reduced the "SF" from 10 to 8 stitches, the four short rows you knitted across the back are equal to half a "SF"...so the "SF"s should still be in phase with each other.

To enable you to cut the hood and the body in two separate bursts, it is a good idea to put the center four "cutting" stitches on a piece of wool, and cast on (by backward loops) 4 new cutting stitches. As an afterthought, we wish we'd done that in the middle of the body as well.

HOOD: Mark the center back 2 stitches (the "sc"), and increase one stitch each side of them every 2nd round, 8 times. We kept the 16 extra stitches in purl. This increasing leaves the base of the hood narrow for the neck, but shapes the back in an organic way. Now work straight to a total height of 12"-13". Put the hood stitches on a piece of wool.

BASTE & MACHINE STITCH the hood and center front of the coat. Keep the stitching very close to the center basting. Cut.

WEAVE the underarms, doing the best you can to match the patterns together.

HOOD EPAULET: Work back and forth on the 4 center-back stitches (the P1, "sc", P1) uniting them to the sides of the hood as you did on the shoulders. When you reach the front, put the 4 raw stitches on a piece of wool to be I-Corded later.

FRONT BORDERS: With right side facing, beginning at lower edge, staying in one chosen vertical row, KNIT UP 2 stitches for every 3 rounds from lower edge to neck.

Work back and forth in garter stitch for 8 ridges (16 rows), slipping all first stitches, and slanting the

This photo shows the slanted front borders, the toggle ties and buttonholes, the firm I-Cord across the inside of the neck back (a Shoulder Holder), and the 2-stitch I-Cord edging around the hood.

171

Here you see the finished pockets, inside and out, and the neatened cut edge.

top edge as follows: At the beginning of ridges #6, 7, and 8, Slip 1, K2 together.

CAST OFF: Use SEWN CASTING OFF *(see appendix)*, our favorite for garter-stitch, and repeat the foregoing on the other side.

Apply **2-Stitch I-Cord** across the slanted top of the front border, around the hood, and across other border.

NEATEN CUT EDGES: Fold the little flap toward the body, tuck the machine-stitched row under the edge, and tack it down with matching sewing thread. *(see photo above)*

SHOULDER HOLDERS: With such thick wool, the sleeves are quite heavy, and may tend to drag and stretch the shoulders. To keep them in place, work a *very firm* I-Cord (attached to every other - or even every third - stitch) across the back, on the inside, from shoulder point to shoulder point, using the 3-ply Sheepswool.

AFTERTHOUGHT POCKETS: Try the coat on, and decide where you want the pockets to be. Refer to Chapter Five (page 77). Work the first few rows of the pocket lining in Sheepsdown, then switch to the lighter weight 3-ply

Sheepswool for the rest of the pocket, to obviate thickness.

TOGGLE TIES: These are great fun to make. Take about a yard of wool (we used the Sheepsdown and the 3-ply Sheepswool together for greater strength), and clamp one end between your knees. Twist the other end until it is so tight that it spins back upon itself. Allow it to do just that, and tie the doubled, twisted strand tightly around the center of a toggle. Check the length of the ends and cut off the excess. Tie knots in each end, and sew them onto the front border.

TOGGLE BUTTONHOLES: With a shorter length of wool, twist as above. Tie it tightly around a film can (or something of that diameter). Knot the ends, and sew onto the opposite border.

BLOCKING: Because this is such a heavy garment, special care must be taken here. Steaming the finished coat gently with a steam-iron is recommended. When the time comes to wash it, the extra weight of the water will pull its sleeves and body quite long. Try to lift it bodily out of the wash (as opposed to pulling it up by the hood), and get it into the machine to spin out the excess water. Arrange it in the machine, (or put it into a pillow case) so that the sleeves and hood will not be stretched by the centrifugal force of the spin cycle. Take it from the machine, and block as usual.

173

. . . Digressions

Thomas, having just raked the leaves, standing in front of 2010 E. Wood Place. c. 1950

When I first met the house on 2010 E. Wood Place, Shorewood, Wisconsin, I sat down in its spacious living room and wept. To live in a prosperous Milwaukee suburb after several years on the beautiful Pennsylvania-side of the Delaware river sandwiched between it and the historic Delaware Canal took some doing. But character pulled itself together, and before long the suburb of Shorewood proved to be idyllic. The lakeshore, good schools, nice shops, and again friendly neighbors. Upon first arrival, the Zimmermann kids were getting acquainted with a gang of Hainer kids over the back fence, and somebody said provocatively, "My mother says 'Dammit to hell'," and somebody from the other side said proudly, "My mother says 'Dammit to hell' too!" after which both gangs streaked back into their respective houses to tell the news. And so my friendship with Ruth Hainer was born before we ever met. After a time Ruth was joined by several other Shorewood women into what we called the Sewing Ladies, which formed almost immediately, and there we sat in one of our living rooms every single Thursday, mending or sewing or knitting and chattering away like a TV sitcom.

The local knitshop, owned and run by Sophie, also provided plenty of chatter and wool, which for me was especially useful and beguiling. I spent morning after morning in there meeting local knitters, dropping little hints on them, and,

Elizabeth and her first "knitted" car. 1958

best of all, absorbing their hints. Helping them with some of their puzzles and troubles almost caused me to write an actual knitting book (this occurred several years later - 1971, *Knitting Without Tears*), and certainly taught me what a sad knitting-life many knitters led, dependent on knitting *instructions*. These consisted chiefly of magazine articles which took for granted that their readers were familiar with technically-expressed and abbreviated "directions", and were capable knitters to start with. Thus, when I submitted my Norwegian designs to *Woman's Day* in 1955, I

174

remember being careful to write the instructions like a KNITTING-human-being, describing this homely skill clearly, kindly, and completely. Other knitting magazines, *McCalls* and *Vogue Knitting*, by whom I subsequently had designs accepted, fueled my ambitions as a knitting designer, but, as outlined in chapter two, I soon became annoyed by editors who felt it their duty to translate my style and designs back into the standard, two-needle technical blather. So by fits and starts, with mail on the subject starting to flow in, I decided to start my own regular hand-knitting publication in 1959. This has continued to this very day, and has been ineffably bolstered by our clever daughter Meg's assistance and ability since 1965.

It was also in the late fifties that we obtained our beloved Schoolhouse. You should have seen the place the first day we did. We went there with the Lambs, as Bob Lamb was very kindly offering to show us around Wood County, a wild part of agricultural central Wisconsin, with the object of finding us about 40 acres as a hideout (beautiful American word). We saw a couple of bits of land and then we came to this one. As we turned in the road I said to Arlene Lamb, "I believe this one has a derelict schoolhouse on it," and she pronounced the historic words, "Oh, you wouldn't want THAT". She should have known better, if she had given a damn, that

is. At this distance, I can no longer say if it was those fighting words that sold us on the place, or the first sight of the little house, forgotten, and blinking philosophically in the early Fall sun. The door was open and it had been freely used, apparently, by hunters and rainbound fishermen. The tall school-windows were almost intact, though, and the litter was awe-inspiring. The previous owner - Floyd Ross - had, it seems, blown his brains out there, and I think it must have been the insoluble problem of the floor that drove him to it. Half of it had been very

Elizabeth, Arnold and Schoolhouse. 1976

neatly and effectively raised against flooding by the nearby Yellow River, and the original boards relaid. Then it must have struck him that the logical result of a complete raising would be that he would be floored in, as neither door would be able to be opened - inwards at least. So he drank a quart of whiskey and released himself from this vale of tears. As far as we know, he doesn't haunt, though.

The unraised floor was in waves as a result of a flood rotted, sub-floor and the ghastly green ceiling was completely stained from the leaking roof. We gave each other a look, commented knowingly on these drawbacks, and allowed as how we wanted it. The Lambs were thunderstruck, but Bob immediately rallied, and offered to bargain for us. So we searched out a man called Gray, who had bought it for a song for taxes, promised Bob to keep our traps tightly shut, and listened in on a simply classic piece of bargaining. Such haggling, such tearful pleading, such scorn of the offers Lamb and Gray threw at each other, I never in this life expect to hear again. They both thoroughly enjoyed themselves, and Bob beat the price down from 2400 to 1850, which was a fine profit for Gray and a fine saving for us. Good old Bob. So then we kissed our schoolhouse *Aufwiedersehen* and waited out the winter while the conventions of title-searching, etc, were being completed. Early in the spring we started to go on weekends. It was so foul that for the first couple of times Arnold wouldn't sleep there, and we stayed in a cabin north of Babcock, our closest town (population all of 300 +). It was there that we first met a chunk-stove, and became enamored of it, and this started a mighty hunt for one of our own.

The floor had been raised 14", which is conveniently just two steps, so we continued to raise it until 3/4 was up and 1/4, where the doorway is, down. It was a herculean job, and Arnold and Lloie had to put in a completely new subfloor and joists for it. As Arnold took up the maple floor-boards, he piled them under the east window until they reached a disgusting pile right up to the sill. And I do mean disgusting. That floor had been taking a frightful beating since the school was built in 1916, and the only attention it had received had been repeated coats of shellac. Each one had to be cleaned by hand, and the sandy dirt rapidly blunted the sharpest chisels. I quite truly thought we would never be done, all through the summer of '59 and the following winter and spring. But finally the last board was laid, and we rented ourselves a sander. I think it was Meg with us that weekend, and we worked like dogs. Then it was done and Minwaxed. At first, of course, we wouldn't even walk on it except in stocking feet, but now we have become hardened.

Next, we lowered the ceiling. Originally, it had been about 12' high, and in very poor shape, besides wasting a great deal of heat. We both like low ceilings, and after considerable cogitation, we decided on plain, pine boards, as we had had in the Gardnerville kitchen. The span we had to bridge was enormous, as the schoolhouse is 24' by 28', but the clever Arnold did this without any center supports. The 24' joists were hung in galvinized shoes which we attached to the side beams, and he did make two rows of hanging contraptions between the old and the new ceiling. Tom was there for the first few courses, and with his height it went fast, but from then on it slowed down, and took several weekends. But it, too, was a noble job, and with the walls painted white, looked truly magnificent.

Meanwhile, another kind and fortunate prop to my promotion of handknitting was given by Beulah Donahue, a fellow-member of the Milwaukee Walrus Club, and a daily star on a 15 minute local Milwaukee morning TV show. She invited me to be a guest one day, and the resulting reaction of their listeners almost staggered the correspondence department. Inspired by this, I approached the Milwaukee Educational TV outfit, and suggested to them that I commence a program on handknitting. They were delightfully agreeable, and I plunged in. The result was *The Busy Knitter* in 1964; 10 half hour shows in black and white starring me and Kline, our Siamese cat, who from the start seemed to assume that he would be included. I would take him down to the studio in a picnic basket and then he would pad around, and peer into the camera and generally do what he pleased, not unlike

176

Elizabeth giving a workshop. 1986

what I was doing. Anyway, the series which concentrated on a seamless Raglan pullover/cardigan seemed to go over so well, that *Busy Knitter II* was taped, this time 13 half hours in color, about a Norwegian Drop-Shouldered Sweater. These shows were later lent to other stations in cities all around the US, so maybe some of you who read this are doing so because you saw it. They certainly were instrumental in contributing to the growing number of subscribers to my Newsletter, and now the subsequent *Wool Gatherings*, which Meg and I put out twice a year.

As I mentioned at the beginning of this chapter, Barbara Walker was responsible for getting me in touch with Scribner's and my wonderful editor, Eleanor Parker. *Knitting Without Tears*, which I wanted to call The Opinionated Knitter, was written during 1970 and published in 1971, and is still in print at this writing. Meg tells me that it has set some kind of a record at Scribner's as being their first "how-to-book" to remain in continuous print for eighteen years (and counting). Also, by the late 60's and 70's, I was doing knitting appearances (workshops) in all imaginable directions, and even now in the 80's as far away as New Zealand. In a more formal setting, The University of Wisconsin, through Charlene and Bob Burmingham, organized what we call Knitting Camp, in 1974 at Shell Lake, Wisconsin. Camp continued in the 80's in Marshfield Wisconsin, and last summer (1988) was Meg and my 15th year of Camp. I'm convinced that I learn as much as my victims at each session.

Arnold and I are now entering the ultimate stage of long, and certainly happy lives. In the beginning years it is nothing but struggle; physical, mental, spiritual. When I see these pretty, haggard young mothers in the grocery store, my heart goes out to them in a perfectly unnecessary fashion. Unnecessary, because they are much too driven and bedevilled and enjoying themselves to have any idea that they might inspire pity. There they are, hardly out of their teens, one baby in the grocery basket, two clutching their skirts, one probably to be fetched from grade school before they steam home to fix meals which will be mostly left on plates for Mother to eat up so that it will not be wasted. Then there is the young and probably anxious husband to coddle and reassure. After all, he is responsible for this circus to which there seems no end, and the insurance people lose no opportunity to remind him what a fix they would be left in should God forbid. Yet these women are so *necessary* that they just shine, and what greater happiness is there than that? I really think I think that. Isn't being necessary the greatest form of earthly bliss? Necessary to the family for the wife or husband; to the Lord in doing His will for the priest; necessary to the plant for the businessman; necessary to culture for the artist; and finally necessary to himself for

Elizabeth reading to Meg, Thomas and Lloie. Christmas 1944.

the philosopher. Is this a facile philosophy, or is it one of the flashes of intelligence that I am hoping will illuminate these pages of discursive rambling? No, I think I'm on to something good - at least to a source of fruity and possibly fruitful argument.

Looking back, it is the sympathy, companionship, practice, expertness, the faculty of adaptation, familiarity, and, as someone perspicacious said , the shattering things one has gone through together that represent love to me. (What a German sentence!) But because one has gone through them together, they are not shattering. Remembering the rather awful things we have experienced, I cannot recall being really scared at the time, so that they are awful only in retrospect, which is not awful at all. Imagine waiting all those years to get married, and then being married with no job and no money, and then to come to America, still jobless, and living in that really rather scary Richmond Hill, and when Tom licked the ant-buttons and nearly had it, and when he ate the deadly nightshade and nearly had it again. And the winter before Meg was born, in Gardnerville without even a sink and with two small children. Every drop of water for cooking, washing, and dishes, had to be first brought up out of the outside well in a bucket, used, and then carried out to be emptied. Pots had to be carried to the little half-moon hotel. Apples froze in the next room. A wet diaper would freeze to the floor; a wet bed would freeze when the child was taken out of it. But we were quite cheerful. We didn't even have a radio, and only a handful of books. But I read *Little Women* over and over again. And then there was Lloie's dog-bite, and she nearly had it, and losing the job in Pennsylvania, and later on my OPERATIONS and the accompanying dreads, along with the various amours of the kids to be assessed for their full shock value. And of course, all the while poor Arnold's frightful apprehensions and fears at being the head and responsible for this whole gang, and being German, he is easy prey for apprehensions at the most peaceful of times. He must have gone through hell. At this stage, I am in a position to remind him of past occasions and how his dreads have been so rarely realized, but in those days I had no such backlog of experience to cite to him, and he had to take my Cheerful Charley stuff on trust. Anyway, I think I can truly say that all these things didn't bother us nearly so much at the time as they do in retrospect. In fact, we were so busy coping with them that they didn't bother us at all except in a practical sense. Goddammit, it's all in the mind! If you keep on assuring yourself this is ridiculous, of course such things don't happen to me, they don't. But if you say constantly, Ah, DOOM again, just what I was expecting, then Pandora's box just turns itself upside down on top of you, and you wallow in a welter of woes.

And finally, what about our new country America? America is not better, but different. That difference makes it better for me in a personal sense, but I certainly don't expect everybody to share my opinion. Damn these people, whose parents went through untold agonies to come to the New World away from the prejudice and self-importance of the old. They are now just as self-important themselves. They are so convinced of the superiority and delights of their fifty states that they quite truly believe that everybody on the terrestrial sphere envies them. May I say the thought staggers me. Of course it's a splendid country; of course I love it dearly, but there are other countries no less splendid, or shall we say no less faulty, and their inhabitants love them dearly too. And that is to the credit of all concerned, until it comes to the point of thinking that there can only be **one** splendid country, namely one's own. That's where the prejudice, nationalism, and intolerance of all kinds tends to breed. What do I mean tends, it does breed, and our main job is to smite it, hip and thigh. The only way I can see this done is to have our children so mixed around the globe, that they can learn, and also prove to others, that all people are alike, good and bad mixed. I have lived for extended periods now in three countries. For the first eighteen years in England, where I absorbed the facts - uncontrovertible ones - that the English were Top People, hand-picked by God to rule the world, and that all the natives were so *grateful* to us for doing the dirty work of ruling them; that it was our unpleasant, but bound and Christian duty, to spread out over the world, dispensing the British way of life.

With this state of mind firmly fixed, I then spent seven years studying and living in Germany. Here it was gradually, and I must say rather painfully, borne upon me that I had been criminally misled, and that the poor, deluded English were mistaken in believing themselves the cream of the crop. All the time it was the Germans who were the chosen people; talented, fleissig, noble, and supremely fitted to govern the lesser breeds, in which God-given destiny the nefarious, perfidious British had frustrated them. So, I allowed as how the Germans were quite right about their being owners of the best country the world had yet produced, and I may say this fitted in very well with my own plans, as I had quite decided to marry one of them, and it was nice to know that I could go right on being one of the Top People.

Now comes the extraordinary coincidence. Though still decided to marry my German, circumstances made it desirable, nay, inevitable, that we emigrate to the New World. We settled down as best we could, and as soon as we began to peer

179

Knitter's Bliss. Lac Seul, Canada. 1986

around us it became perfectly obvious that the poor Germans had to join the poor British as victims of the hallucination that they had been called upon to lead. Why, by gosh, all the time it had been the United States. Sticks out like a sore thumb. How could I have been so blind? Well. I'm sure even the least intelligent would at this point have begun to smell a rat. I keep pretty quiet about it, though perhaps not as quiet as I should, in the interests of general amity.

Be all this as it may... in reviewing my 79 years on this globe, I look with gratifying wonder at the Kaleidoscopic sequence of events that have led to my present quiet retirement in our secluded backwater. My childhood is highlighted by personal attachments: My father, my aunts on both my parent's sides are a lasting wonderful impression. My times spent at the seaside; at the farm of my Auntie Pete; the memories of not quite comprehended uneasy feelings about the first war - my Father in the Navy, uncles in the Air Corps and in the trenches in France, and the Zeppelin attacks on London. School days in the small private school in Westgate; the time in our bungalow in Birchington and the daily walks along the beach in all its ebb tide miracles. Our stay in Brightlingsea, when my father was stationed there - how these memories jumped out of time's dusty closets on our several recent visits: just like a jack-in-the-box.

Then the after-the-war years with my mother managing "Meals By Motor"; an uneasiness in my young life. Boarding School, something I had to live through, but which gave me the true friendship of Marge Smardon. Then the pensionnat in Lausanne. Art school there, and relative freedom, which fostered self-reliance. Munich - a thoroughly new, exciting and unexpected world. My years at the Hey-mannschule, where I really learned how to paint and draw. Then the passing of the

180

entrance-exam into the Munich Academy of Fine Arts, attending the class of Prof. Hess. And in 1930, I met Arnold. How can true love open so many hitherto unknown doors in one's soul? A miraculous change in the concept of life's purpose. The long years of our engagement. Happy years, and yet concerned with the uncertainty of the future over shadowed by the political developments in Germany.

And finally, after many obstacles, our marriage and our voyage into a new country and a new life - our life. Children, Knitting, and success with my books about it. From the East to the Midwest, exploring Wisconsin on weekend camping-trips with tent and boat. Finding our Schoolhouse, rebuilding it and extending it - all done by ourselves.

Retirement, grandchildren - I've had good innings, and may I hope to have more. If you drop a stitch, pick it up immediately!

Good Knitting—

Elizabeth.

Elizabeth and Arnold, sitting beneath Arnold's mural in the dining room of 2010 E Wood Place, the day they retired to the Schoolhouse.

APPENDIX

The following are techniques used in this book, the instructions for which are not included in the text. They are all clearly demonstrated on the video.

(CASTING ON)

There are many dozens of ways to Cast On, and I encourage you to check one of the many "technique-only" knitting books on the market today.

LONG TAIL (also called Two-Strand):

With the "ball" wool over your forefinger, and the end over your thumb, aim the needle down behind the traversing wool between thumb and finger, twist and turn it upright. This *twist* is stitch #1 (we do not like to make knots in our knitting, and this eliminates the traditional "slip knot" beginning). Now,* pull the needle down and towards you, and you will see a loop form in front of the thumb. Put the needle up into the loop from below, hook the forefinger strand down through the loop, release the thumb, and tighten the stitch onto the needle. Repeat from *.

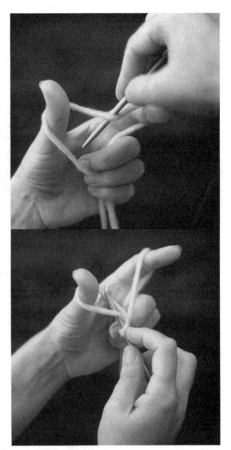

INVISIBLE CASTING ON:

Once mastered, you will find countless uses for this technique. In reality, you are simply winding the working wool (WW) around the needle, separating the loops with a strand of spare wool (SW).

Begin by loosely knotting the two wools. Hold the knot and the needle in your right hand. With the SW on top, and the WW below, *dip the needle *in front* of the SW and pick up a loop of the WW. Now dip the needle *behind* the SW and pick up another loop of WW. Repeat from *.

When you need the stitches (for weaving, or knitting on in the opposite direction), simply pull out the SW, and pick up the waiting stitches.

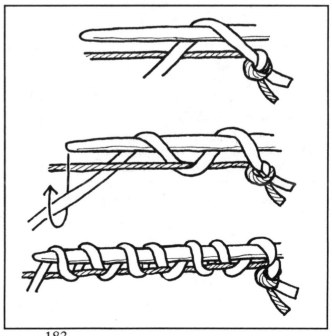

183

K2, P2 CASTING ON

This was bran-new to me a few months ago. It makes a wonderful selvedge for K2, P2 ribbing, and Meg uses it in the video for Beethoven's Variations on a Dickey. We found the technique in KNITTER'S magazine, and reproduce it here with their kind permission.

(KNITTER'S is a Golden Fleece publication. 335 N Main Ave, Sioux Falls, SD)

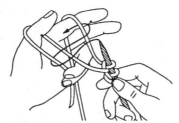

To Knit:1. Arrange both ends of yarn in LH as shown. Bring needle under front strand of thumb loop, up over front strand of index loop, catching it . . .

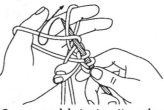

2. . . . and bringing it under the front of the thumb loop. Slip thumb out of loop, and use it to adjust tension on the new stitch.

To Purl: 1. Arrange both ends of yarn in LH as shown. Bring needle behind front strand of index finger loop, behind front strand of thumb loop, up over front strand of index loop, catching it . .

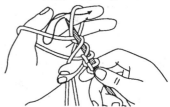

2. . . . and backing it out under the front of the thumb loop. One purl stitch cast on.

(CASTING OFF)

SEWN CASTING OFF:

This is our favorite for use on garter-stitch. It is nice and elastic, as well as good looking. With a *blunt* sewing-up needle, * go through the first two stitches from R to L, go back through the first stitch from left to right, pull the wool through, and slip the stitch off the needle. Repeat from *.

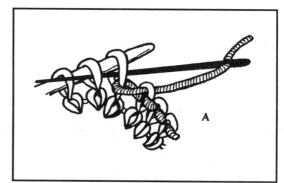

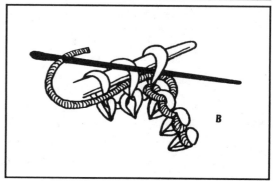

DECREASES

The four I seem to use most often are:

K2 tog: Dig the R needle into the second stitch on the L needle, and knit the two stitches together.

Sl 1, K1, psso: Slip one knitwise, knit one, pass the slipped stitch over the knit stitch.

K2 tog tbl: With the R needle, go into the back of the next two stitches on the L needle and knit them together.

SSK: Barbara Walker alerted most knitters to this. It is a mirror-image of K2 tog, and most useful when working decreases in pairs. However, another knitter, Dee Barrington, came up with a slight variation, which we find even more pleasing.

Barbara's original instructions told us to slip 2 stitches knitwise (one at a time), insert the tip of the left hand needle into the slipped stitches, and knit them together.

Dee tells us to slip the first stitch knitwise, but *slip the second stitch purlwise,* and proceed as above. Try them both in very thick wool, and you can see a slight improvement with Dee's method; slipping as if to purl tucks the second stitch neatly in behind the first.

I-CORD

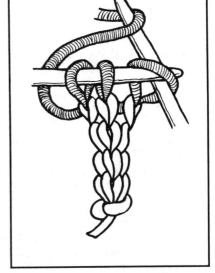

BASIC I-CORD: Cast on three stitches. *Knit three, replace onto lefthand needle, and repeat from *. This produces a tiny tube of stocking stitch. Most of the variations on this I-Cord are explained in KNITTING WORKSHOP, but we keep coming up with (and hearing of) new twists. See Chapters 4 & 5 of this book.

TWO-STITCH I-CORD: The same as above, but on just two stitches; particularly good as Applied I-Cord in thick wool.

SQUARE I-CORD: The same as above, but K1, P1, K1.

INCREASES

I really only use three of the myriad increases available, and two of them are variations of "make one":

M(ake) 1: Make a backward loop over the right hand needle...a half-hitch. If you are increasing in pairs, you may choose to face them in opposite directions. For this, I make one over my finger, and the other over my thumb. On the next round, knit into the front of A, but into the back of B.

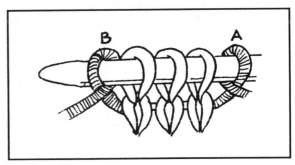

185

"M1" VARIATION: This is a bit tidier than making a loop over the needle, as you are actually making one in the preceding round, and, by borrowing wool from each neighbor stitch, it is firmer and less noticeable:

From the back, pick up the running thread between the two stitches, put it on the L needle. Now, you want to twist it to prevent a hole, so knit into either the front or the back of it, depending upon which way you put it on the L needle. *(see video)*

K INTO B of ST of ROW BELOW: This is the most invisible increase I know of.

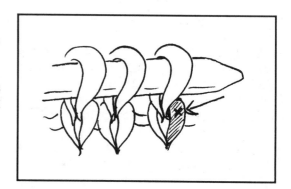

     With the R needle, pick up the R half of the stitch below the next one on the needle (x), put it on the L needle, and knit into the *back* of it.

SHORT ROWS (or WRAPPING)

Short rows are most useful, can be easily tamed, and are rendered all but invisible by using the following technique. Here again, we use a variation on Barbara Walker's original description. This one is from Medrith Glover, and the following instruction applies whether you are on the knit or the purl side of your knitting.

FOR STOCKING STITCH:

     Leaving the working wool where it is, slip the next stitch onto the R needle, take the wool to the other side, replace the slipped stitch. Turn. See how the stitch has been wrapped by the working wool?

     When you next meet the wrap on the Knit side: knit the wrap and the stitch together.

     When you meet the wrap on the purl side: lift the back of the wrap (it will be on the knit side of the work), put it on the L needle, and purl the wrap and the stitch together. *(see video)*

FOR GARTER STITCH:

     Work as above, BUT, when you come to the wrap again, ignore it. It is impossible to hide a short row in garter-stitch (two ridges suddenly become one), but, by leaving the wrap around the stitch, it looks rather like a purl bump, and blends in nicely.

(WEAVING)

Weaving is the essential skill necessary to produce a seamless garment. If you do not know how to weave, I encourage you to knit up a stocking-stitch and a garter-stitch swatch, and practice over and over until you can weave blindfolded.

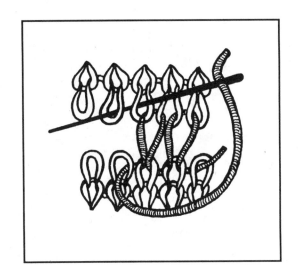

STOCKING STITCH WEAVING:

You are uniting two pieces of fabric with a sewing needle. Be sure to use a *blunt* needle so as not to accidently split the wool. Also, do not worry about tension while you are weaving; keep it loose, and adjust each stitch to match the surrounding fabric after you are finished.

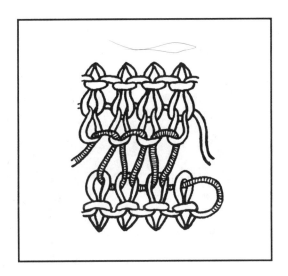

GARTER STITCH WEAVING:

This is a bit tricky in that you must make sure the two pieces to be woven are in the proper relationship to each other. If you stretch garter-stitch apart, you will see horizontal ridges with "valleys" in between. You must have a Ridge up against one needle, and a Valley against the other. NOW, where there is a Ridge, you will weave a Valley; where there is a Valley, you will weave a ridge. When the needle goes "down, up" the result is a Valley (the ridge is on the other side), and when the needle goes "up, down", you will see that you have produced a ridge. *(see video)* Practice.

INDEX